D0721897

ETHNIC CHRONOLOGY SERIES

NUMBER 1

THE AMERICAN INDIAN
1492 - 1976

A Chronology & Fact Book
Second Edition

Compiled and edited by

Henry C. Dennis

Foreword by
Robert L. Bennett

1977
OCEANA PUBLICATIONS, INC.
DOBBS FERRY, NEW YORK

Library of Congress Cataloging in Publication Data

Dennis, Henry C
   The American Indian, 1492-1974.
   (Ethnic chronology series; 1)
   Bibliography: p.
   Includes index.
   SUMMARY: A chronological history of the North American Indians with
a selection of illustrative documents, appendices, and bibliography.
   1. Indians of North America--History--Chronology.
2. Indians of North America--Biography.
[1. Indians of North America--History. 2. Indians of North America--Bi-
ography] I. Title. II. Series.
E77.D393 1976   970'.004'97   76-46440
ISBN   0-379-00526-3

©Copyright 1977 by Oceana Publications, Inc.

Manufactured in the United States of America

To my wife Sally

This book could not have
been written without her
inspiration and help.

CONTENTS

FOREWORD

The chronology of events set out in this publication should provide the public with a ready reference to dates recorded by historians as being dates significant in American Indian history. Since these dates are of significance, the nature of their importance depends upon whether you view them from the Indian perspective or that of the historian. In any case, these events did take place in history, and we live with their effects on the Indian people and, more and more, their effect on the awakening conscience of America. As much as there is a desire to do so, Indian history cannot be changed. Its writing can, however.

We look forward with eager anticipation then to the future writings of Indian history as more and more tribes take on the responsibility of writing their own history as they saw and felt it.

We are beset with so many current problems, however, that the energies of the people of this country, Indian and non-Indian alike, might well be directed to improving the future history of the American Indians rather than dissipating their energies on what may well be valid accusations based upon past history.

The nuances which flow out of the reading of the chronology take the reader from the initial portrayal of the American Indian as benefactor to savage, to pawn, to recipient, and finally to property owner and citizen. Throughout most of it, the assumption is evident that everything done for the Indians was for their own good.

Later events show a more enlightened approach and mark a turning point in the national attitude which is that American Indians must have a voice and be decision makers for their own future.

The prominent Indian figures of the past reflect their natural leadership abilities. This is a select group of famous historical Indian personalities. Most often uneducated by the new world, these figures depict an eminence in leadership qualities whose ideas were imitated by students of government, politics and war in their period of history; coming along in a later environment, the contemporary Indians listed in the sampling applied many ideas first held by the Indians of the past in a sophisticated and acceptable manner. In effect, there appears to be a building on and a continuity of thinking, so that today some of the ideas first espoused by past leaders are now bearing fruit in the present political climate of pluralism.

v

Information follows relating to population in which the one happy fact is the increase in population due to an improved environment and a decrease in infant mortality. The most prominent characteristic of this burgeoning population is its youth, with an estimated 50% under 17 years of age.

The listing of Indian Wars and tribal disturbances is informative except that one may question whose wars they really were.

The list of administrators is significant in that while the last two are Indians, there was only one other Indian on the list and that was some 100 years ago in 1869.

The Government appropriations for Indian education are listed for the years 1877 through 1969. These appropriations have always lagged far behind the costs of even a minimal program. In later years a "catch up" program was started, but it is still a fact today that Indian administration suffers from underfunding. One significant factor is that the appropriation for 1959 of almost $48 million increased in 1969 to $95 1/2 million. This would indicate a doubling of effort on the part of the Congress to invest in Indian education. However, this is not the case as built-in increases in yearly operations account for not less than 80% of the increase in appropriations over that period of time.

The information on Indian museums, Indian groups and a reading and research bibliography are significant and useful to students of Indian history. It might be well to note that Indian groups include both groups made up of Indians and other groups made up of Indians and non-Indians who have an interest in Indian affairs.

While I cannot vouch for the accuracy of the information, I am most happy to attest to the fact that this material is one of the most comprehensive documents of its kind and it should be at the top of the list of any reader who has either an in-depth or casual interest in Indian affairs. Mr. Henry C. Dennis, the author, is to be commended for his diligence and dedication in making this wealth of information available to the public, and Oceana Publications, Inc., is to be complimented for its interest in publishing the material.

ROBERT L. BENNETT

PREFACE

Who are the "Indians"? What is their status in contemporary society? What happened to them after "discovery" and settlement by the Europeans? How has the United States attempted to help these "first Americans"? What is now being done to improve their condition, their acceleration into the "mainstream" of America and their hopes for a better life? These questions plague the thoughtful and concerned American when he views the American Indian scene as we enter the soaring 70's.

This compact chronology and its allied contents historically examine things "as they were" and are. It is not a very pretty or encouraging picture, for despite the fact that more of these American Indians are beginning to taste the sweets of success and attainment, they are still on the lowest rung of the economic ladder in America today.

It is hoped that this book might be read in every home in America, but a more realistic goal would be that it become a used reference source in every library in the country, gradually correcting the twisted picture that is carried in the minds of far too many uninformed palefaced Americans.

The Amerindian has had a very grotesque picture presented of him. Too many historians and writers have provided an image of a savage fighter, which he was, when fighting for his very life, his liberty, his property, and the pursuit of his happiness. Perchance some Hollywood scenario writer will come across this compilation and correct the image fostered by the moving picture industry for far too long.

vii

ACKNOWLEDGMENTS

This book would never have been written had it not been for those students in my Mid-High School (Carlsbad, New Mexico) classes who asked why I did not write American History "as it was." The idea remained in the back of my head, until a chance conversation with Bill Cowan, of Oceana Publications, at the National Council for the Social Studies 1968 Annual Meeting, which lead to this labor of love...a determination to try to re-search the "way it was."

All serious writing must rest upon good research, review and study. I am grateful to two of my former professors, Dr. George W. Smith and Dr. Frank D. Reeve (deceased), for having instilled this in me during my student days at the University of New Mexico. My love for history came to me from my maternal grandfather, Nils J. Walgren, who came to America as a mature immigrant and suffered humiliation from those who had preceded him by a mere generation or two. Also, there are the uncounted and unknown authors and teachers who have given me a background it would be impossible to document, but without whom I might never have written this Chronology.

I wish to express my debt and gratitude to the following persons for their specific help with particular informational quests:

Louis H. Conger, Jr., Chief Statistician, BIA
Richard W. Heim, Administrative Assistant to U.S. Senator
    Clinton P. Anderson
W.S. Buskirk, Captain, U.S. Navy, Special Assistant for
    Liaison and Public Affairs
Thomas J. Kelly, President, Congressional Medal of Honor
    Society
Robert L. Bennett, former Commissioner, BIA
Leo E. Benada, Brigadier General, USA Deputy Assistant
    Secretary of Defense
Dr. James D. Carroll, Division Chief, the Library of Congress
Stepehn A. Lagone, Legislative Reference Service, the Library
    of Congress
B.M. Ettenson, Colonel, USAF, Chief, Congressional Inquiry
    Division, Office of the Secretary of Defense, Department
    of the Air Force
C.A. Stanfiel, Colonel, AGC, Acting the Adjutant General,
    Department of the Army.

A special word of gratitude to Mrs. Leonard Voekler for thoughtful editorial correction of the final manuscript.

LET US BEGIN . . . (Introduction!)

Anthropologists, historians, linguists and writers have advanced a number of theories about American Indian origins...some are reinforced by Indian legends and chants, others by "the old people" or the historians of the tribes, who have orally passed along to the younger generation the lore of the past.

No chronicler like the 20th century space age man noted the exact touchdown by date and minute when the first emigrant from Asia set foot on the North American continent. Nor can we exactly establish when these early ancestors changed their ways from a hunter-fisherman subsistence and began to cultivate the soil. A student of languages suggests the possibility that the first here were the Hokan-Siouian speaking peoples, despite the segmentation and differentiation of languages within that group.

It has been noted that while some peoples of the old world, Hindus, Chinese and the Hellenized, were relatively static and confined to where they lived, the Europeans were always moving, shoving aside frontiers and barriers to eventually dominate all the liveable globe. Such a way of living appears to have created racial adventuring which made men "cocky", imbuing them with a "chosen People" philosophy. By stretching their philosophy, as some men seemingly can do without noting contradiction to human rights, they were able to look down upon others as disposable, and less than human. A prime example is the casual way we call people "natives", mentally removing humanity from them, and then proceed to exterminate or domesticate them without qualms. Many Americans persist in romanticizing the American Indian, or characterizing him into little or nothing of contemporary importance.

Virtually all people of school age and beyond are acquainted with the accepted American version of history concerning Christopher Columbus. While seeking the new passage to India, Columbus mistakenly landed in the Western Hemisphere, and upon discovering his mistake when he met the natives he returned to Europe with the news about the "New World" and the "Indians". The mystery which had to be solved was "how did 'they' get there?" Bit by bit, piece by piece, the puzzle has been worked upon by great minds over the centuries. Today we can present a plausible answer. The story of the Indians' past is not a smooth, connected affair, for many of the essential facts and time sequences are not presently known. Despite this, there appears to be a general acceptance of the evolvement story.

Perhaps the most accepted hypothesis is that ancestors of the modern Indians came from Eurasian origins; they were wandering hunters who drifted over a period of thousands of years in many migrations from Asia. They came across the Bering Strait over a landmass bridge now vanished (although soundings show a depth of a mere 60-100 feet along a possible pathway to a connection with North America), over the frozen tundra, or possibly island-hopping the short sixty mile distance to Alaska in canoes made of animal skins. The walking theory seems to be the most accepted version, for it follows the correlation that the first North Americans were following and hunting the game which preceded them. Some no doubt stopped to rest and recuperate, while others settled permanently.

The initial bands were succeeded by others who meandered down from Alaska through the Western Hemisphere. Over thousands, possibly tens of thousands of years and many waves of migrations, they wandered through what is now the United States, on into Central and South America until they reached the end of the continent at Tierra del Fuego, in Chile. The animals they hunted left huge prints, and fossil remains of mastodons, camels, horses and similar ice-age creatures have since been found in tar pits, in drained lakes and in lava beds.

There can be few men who would discount the thesis that the hunters were also investigators and curious about their new environment. New trees, bushes and vegetation had to be tasted with, no doubt, occasional deadly results as well as salubrious effects, until after a time the Indians learned to cultivate the good and avoid the harmful. The meanderers kept a stream of information and results flowing back and forth to the more sedentary groups who became the Pueblo farmers, the seed gatherers, the desert dwellers and the shepherds. The news of the storage possibilities of corn as a way to avoid period of drought no doubt permitted the planters to keep alive from the ravages of nature and from the attacks of other men. Stronger men gradually absorbed the weaker ones, and from such unions a stronger species emerged and adapted to the land. The less adventurous took to town living, while the wanderers spread out across the plains, some becoming the woodsmen of the eastern forests and others the northern fishermen. There were cycles of a sort and contra-cycles, each adding a bit to what had come before.

Radiocarbon dating, dendrochronology techniques and other devices fill in the general outlines of earlier researchers, but new findings merely support earlier evidence in the form of skeletal remains, pottery, housing, weaponry, etc., examined in the past. Despite some arguments about the exact dates when men first existed in the Americas, no one at the time of this writing seems to hypothesize beyond 30,000 years ago.

The first materials showing early man were found in the Sandia
Cave, just a few miles east of present-day Albuquerque, New Mexico, in
the Sandia Mountains. The oldest archaeological evidence of any early
culture was found near northeastern New Mexico and given the name of
Folsom. Materials similar to that of Folsom were also found at nearby
Clovis, New Mexico, and not far away at Fort Collins, Colorado, and
Lipscomb, Texas. This evidence was in the form of projectile points of
two types; one rough and irregular and the other very minutely chipped
and fine. Some of these which had been points were found sticking in the
bones of age-old bison, preserved for our modern wonderings over the
ages. (A word of caution must be given: the mere connection of man-
made artifacts with now extinct animals does not, ipso facto, mean any
long-term history.) The Folsom people apparently were hunters, and their
gifts to history consist merely of scrappers, knives, and projectile points.
Another later group, the Chochise culture appears to have centered around
southern Arizona. Subsequent cultures appear to have merely added to
the aforementioned two cultures, principally with pottery making and improvements in agriculture and housing. The nearer we come to the present, the more evidence we uncover to support theories and to make them
acceptable.

There is another viewpoint which conceptualizes human origin on
this continent as being in Old Mexico, possibly from persons who came
from Africa or the Orient by floating across the Atlantic Ocean on rafts
equipped with crude sails. From Mexico these people moved north, by
slow stages, into the present United States and Canada. This they may
have done after creating the impressive government and strong religion
which was in Mexico when the Europeans arrived. Thus, the connection
between gulf region and inland groups which we find reflected in ideas,
art, religious practices and legends leading to the possible link of the
Mound Builders and the Aztec temples may be explained. The African
raft theory may not be so remote, for in the summer of 1970 the adventurous Scandinavian Thor Heyerdahl (Kon Tiki fame) completed a 3,200
mile journey by crude balsa log rafts, which started out from Africa and
ended in Barbados, Bridgomonn, in the Caribbean.

It is fascinating to talk with scientists and to note how lucidly they
project their ideas and cite techniques to tie in their thoughts about the
Sandia Man, the Folsom Man, the Minnesota Woman, the Basket Makers,
the Anazi, the Hohokam and the Mogollon cultures. They will readily
admit, however, that several items are missing from the jigsaw puzzle
which are needed to "nail down" their theories beyond a shadow of a doubt.

Outstanding and obvious is the lack of a written record. Some
caves with petroglyphs, pictographs and other crude markings of early man

would seem to indicate his presence many thousands of years ago. But skeletal remains and artifacts, such as points and pottery, have never been found together. There is not complete agreement as to the exact age of the findings, although all are ancient by "new world" standards, 10-15-25-30,000 years, more or less. There are those who refute the radiocarbon dating, or the tree ring dating methods, by which may be determined the ebb and flow of ice flows, or the wet and dry periods. It is not the purpose of this writer to agree or disagree, but rather to bring to the reader more verifiable contact and communication. Suffice it to say, the various theories make fascinating listening, reading and conjecture. To repeat: many of these theories are supported by Indian legends.

The Indians enjoyed a religion and civilization that may have reached its zenith about the year 1,000. Certainly, like today's world, where there are some groups and nations more fortunate than others, there must have been some tribes who were more advanced than other Indian nations. Even to a casual observer they left an eloquent account of their history and civilization in now-deserted dwellings and in their burial grounds, in their vanished campgrounds and "pueblos". Buried art work in the form of pottery, ornaments and baskets rivals artistic work of modern-day American craftsmen. The primitive peoples wove wild cotton and hair into garments and made baskets of grass, willows and wood. From clay they fashioned household utensils, and they created ornaments from bones, feathers, shells, teeth and stones. They had underground mines long before the arrival of the white newcomer and they brought forth beauty from the ground in their earth-toned frescoes which adorned kivas and similar places of worship.

The first Americans looked upon nature as the source of all existence, and they revered it. They constructed their religion around nature using the sun, earth, rain, sky, mountains and plains to provide incentives to worship. Religion was the very center of their existence and they built their daily lives about it, praying continuously to the powers and expressing their thanks and wishes through their dances. Notwithstanding the modern Christian's claim to conversion of the Indian, those who know and love the Indians recognize that it is but a surface allegiance and that basically the Indian religion is still paramount for the majority of red men. For instance, the medicine man is still a vital part of the life of the Navajos, and no man who has had business dealings with them would think of opening a new building without having a "blessing" sung by the mystic's Indian equivalent of the white man's Dr. Albert Schweitzer.

Countless centuries have gone by since the Indians came to the Americas and at least five centuries, possibly ten, have elapsed since the coming of the white man. Only in the southwestern part of the United States have Indians in large numbers kept to the ways of their ancestors, maintaining their faith and traditions on their reservations and in their pueblos. Sometimes, and ins ome places, they have been inescapably driven to new ways of life.

As in ancient times when there were two groups of Indians, today their equivalent counterparts still exist in our 20th century nuclear/space/ computer life. There was the restless hunter/nomad who peopled the bountiful plains, moving with the game and the sun. Even in the desert today some of these fierce and hardy types can be found in the Apaches and the Navajos. Once deathly feared by white and red man alike, they are now reduced to a passive life of herding cattle and sheep on reservations. The other groups were the farmers who tilled the soil when first contacted by the white man on the eastern shore and earlier by the Spanish, in their peaceful pueblos or villages. Each should be considered separately since their way of life was, and is, different. The pueblos no doubt have resisted the advances of the white man's time, and in many Indian villages today there are no great changes.

In spite of the automobile, which even today many do not own, life in a pueblo is unhurredly peaceful and calm. Some still lack modern conveniences and sanitation, but the pueblos are remarkably clean and quiet. Women still bake in their outdoor ovens, and each spring they mud-paint their homes.

It should be pointed out that there is no "Indian language", there are no common physical characteristics and no organized Indian religion. Like their white American counterparts with known European roots, Indians are mixtures in origin and they were adaptive to the climate, country and conditions under which they were forced to live.

It has been estimated that when Columbus first met the "Indians", there were between 900,000 and 1,000,000 living in what was to become the United States.

The once-fashionable phrase "the vanishing Red Man" arose from a comparison of the United States Census of 1880, which showed 250,000, with the Columbus estimate. The conclusion of racial extinction was reached. That trend has now reversed itself with a 1969 estimate of 650,000 persons claiming to be American Indians.

CHRONOLOGY

3000 years ago: The earliest known farmers in North America were part of the longest continuous cultural line of what is called the "Cochise Culture" of southern Arizona and New Mexico. They raised a very primitive form of corn 3000 years ago. From this culture, in the course of a thousand years or so, derived the Mogollon and the Hohokam cultures; and from the Hohokam people, it is believed, the modern Pimas are in part descended.

1000 years ago: Somewhere about this time it is believed that the Norsemen contacted the Micmac Indians, an Algonquin Tribe, thereby making the first white/red encounter on the northeast coast of America.

1492 At the time of European discovery of America by Columbus there were about 300 different languages spoken by the Indians, and the number of Indians was estimated to be 840,000. This contrasts greatly with the 19th century figure of 243,000, a 1960 census count came to 552,000, including 28,000 Aleuts and Eskimos in what is now the United States.

1497 The English explorer, Sebastian Cabot, came into contact with the Micmac Indians and returned to England with three of them. The tribe can be found today living in Canada.

1500 or 1501 Gaspar Corte Real, Portuguese explorer, told of his kidnapping more than fifty Indians who were then sold into slavery.

1524 The initial kidnapping in the New World was noted in a letter dated July 8th sent to King Francis I of France by Verrazano, the Italian explorer. In detailing his findings in America, it was revealed that his crew took a child (Indian) from an old woman. At the same time they attempted to abduct a "young and beautiful woman of tall stature." She screamed, however, and scared the abductors into changing their minds and intentions, so they left her behind.

1528 Europeans first viewed the Karankawa Indians of Texas when the survivors of a Spanish shipwreck managed to get ashore on the Gulf Coast. Half-starved, the white men appalled the Indians by eating the bodies of men of their ship who were washed up on the beach. The Karankawas drew the line at eating members of their own tribe.

1532   Indians are "the true owners of the 'New World', " said Francisco de Vetoria in a communication to Spanish Emperor Charles V.

1535   Spanish explorer Cabeza de Vaca, writing in his journals of his explorations in the territory which is now New Mexico, told about the pinon nuts, "sweeter than the nuts of Spain, stored away for the winter by the Indians to be used as a delicacy and food when snows cover the ground. "

1540   On July 7th, the die was cast for the Spanish and the Zuni Indians to live relatively peacefully side by side. A short battle with the Zuni by Francisco de Coronado, who led a small band of soldiers at Hawikuh, resulted in the friendliness of the Zuni.

Spanish records verify that ancestors of the Hopi lived in the states at that time. (Archeologists have tried to carry Hopi genealogy through the pueblo dweller back to the cave dwellers.)

The Spanish explorers mentioned "Querechos," "Teyas," and "Paducahs," found in the plains region; natives who, unlike the pueblo peoples, lived in skin tents, used dogs as beasts of burden, and hunted for their food.

1568   Jesuit Fathers from Cuba organized a school of Havana for Indian children from Florida. This school was the first school attended by Indian children who lived within the United States.

1570   League of Six Nations formed. After a long period of tribal warfare over the rich lands of central New York, certain Iroquois chiefs had come to realize that, in the long run, everyone benefited from peace. Included in the group were the Mohawks, Oneidas, Senecas, Cayugas and Onondagas. Later on new tribes were taken into the league, although they did not speak the Iroquois language. There was a council which guided the league, directed by fifty Sachems, or wise men. When a Sachem passed on to the Happy Hunting Grounds, his replacement was appointed by the chief from the same tribe. The Council regulated inter-tribal matters of war and peace.

1582-   An early-day explorer, Gallegos, found that all of the Zuni
1583   valley was cultivated, and "that not a grain of corn is lost." (Corn and other grains were stored scrupulously during harvest to avoid periods of famine during droughts.)

1583   The term Zuni is first noted to have been used by Antonio de Espejo, when referring to the Ashiwi. Presumably he made use of a Kerean designation, for the Laguna people called them "Sunyitsi," and it is noted that other Keres-speakers used that word with slight differences of dialect.

1584   Raleigh's expedition to North America, under command of Ballow and Amadas, landed along the Carolina coast. Here they met Grangamimeo, brother of Wingina, the local chief of Indians. Despite the lack of common language, it was learned that they were not the first white men in the area. A ship had been wrecked there three years earlier. The survivors had lived with the natives before trying to get home again in their rowboats. This was the explanation for the numerous red-haired Indian children.

1585   Raleigh's second expedition to the New World was a near disaster, with the participants being saved by the chance arrival of the great English sea warrior. Aside from records and drawings, nothing was brought back except a new vegetable called the potato, which was destined to become a staple food for Europeans.

            Sir Richard Grenville was hospitably received by the Indians when he landed in Virginia. When one silver cup was stolen, presumably by an Indian, he repaid the warm welcome by burning and plundering their village. (Indians state that the cup was merely misplaced, and was not made of silver but of tin!)

1587   Manteo became the first Indian convert who was baptized into the Church of England on August 13th, by Sir Walter Raleigh.

1589   The attempt to keep out non-Indians failed when an expedition ventured into the land of the pueblos. Four hundred Spanish men, women and children wound their way through the land in a long party of over eighty wagons and 7,000 head of assorted livestock.

16th Century   The League of the Five Nations, composed of the Senecas, Onondagas, Mohawks, Cayugas and Oneidas, formed and founded a strong union which kept its vigor until after the American Revolutionary War. In a vague form it is still in existence today.

1605   Tisquantum, better known as "Squanto," and four other Indians were kidnapped by Captain George Waymouth and taken to England to provide information about the "New World".

1607   English settlers in Jamestown Colony were the recipients of much help from the Indians. Led by Powhattan, the Indians gave the early settlers corn and showed them how to plant tobacco. This chief's desire for peace, when combined with the wisdom and tact of Captain John Smith, helped insure and implement that worthy aim in a New World.

            The initial Indian war of any significance occurred in Virginia, on May 27.

1609   Captain John Smith crowned Chief Powhattan of the powerful Algonquin Confederacy as king of the territory around the London Company's Colony of Virginia. Rare diplomacy was thereby shown the Indians, who, even by this early date, had been repeatedly victimized by the early white explorers and colonizers.

            Manhattan Indians attacked Henry Hudson while he was returning from exploring the river which bears his name.

1611-   Although a few Jesuit priests had been in Florida in the 1500's,
1700's   and for a time in the Southwest, their most fertile and fervid times were in this period. Their activities centered around the St. Lawrence River, the Great Lakes, the Mississippi, and their tributaries. Not content with converting the Indians to Christianity, the Jesuits followed a mandate "to educate children of the Indians in the French manner" from King Louis XIV, who rendered them much financial assistance. Some writers insist that their learning was centered toward the conventional academic subjects and French customs, while others contend that the curriculum included, among other subjects, agriculture, carpentry, and handicrafts.

1614   John Rolfe, of the Jamestown colony, was married in April to Pocahontas. Pocahontas had been kidnapped and brought to the new white settlements at Henrko by white men when her father, Powhattan, was away from the village. The marriage was performed with the sanction of the great Indian chief.

1615   The French, under Champlain, were able to breech an elaborate defense fortification, terrify the Onondagos and capture their villages. This was the origin of the Iroquois hatred of the French and may ultimately have cost the French their North American Empire.

1617 On March 24, King James I of England required the Anglican clergy to collect money "for the erecting of some churches and schools for ye education of ye children of these Barbarians in Virginia."

1618 The Directors of the Virginia Company ordered the Governor of their colony to choose a convenient place for the building of "a college for the children of the Infidels." From this mandate 10,000 acres of land were set aside. The ruling House of Burgesses ordered that a stipulated number of Indian boys should be educated. A sizeable sum of money was gathered in England and in the colony to build a college, but an Indian uprising in 1622 killed the movement.

1619 The colonial assembly at Jamestown decreed that any settlers who permitted the Indians "any shooting piece, (sic) shot, powder, or any arms, offensive or defensive," would be hanged.

1620 The New England Bay Colony at Plymouth would have suffered, starved, and died out, had it not been for the generosity of the Indians. Squanto educated the white men in constructing housing and in planting corn.

1621 A defensive alliance between Massasoit, war chief of the Wampanoags, and the Pilgrims in behalf of King James I, was made on April 1, at Strawberry Hill (Plymouth, Mass.). The provisions of this agreement were faithfully kept by both sides for more than half a century.

   Massasoit, Chief of the powerful Wampanoags who controlled the territory of which Massachusetts and Rhode Island were a part, concluded a treaty with the Pilgrims on March 22. By its terms, this treaty for the first time gave land freely to the white man. It was not long before this generosity to the white man was regretted.

1622 On Good Friday, March 22, the main body of settlers at Jamestown were saved from an Indian massacre planned by Opechanough. Having lost a night's sleep, a Christianized Indian lad, Chanco, who lived with Richard Pace, his white godfather, alerted the settlers as to the plot planned against the entire colony. The Indian leader was able, however, to make good his plans in outlying settlements.

The first registered Indian massacre of white people occurred on March 22 at Jamestown, where 347 of the total population of 1,240 were murdered.

1626   Manhattan Island of New York State (part of today's New York City) was sold on May 6 by Shinnecock Indians to the Dutch, led by Governor Peter Minuit, for the equivalent of $24.

At the ceremonies marking the tri-centenary of that event, Chief Thunderbird of Long Island went to Manhattan and offered to buy the island back for the original price!

1629   After a period of intermittent missionary activity in the South-west area, the padres established a permanent mission in Hawikuh. At that time there were six pueblos in Zuniland, New Mexico. Another was soon built at Halona, in a part of today's location of Zuni. Some Indians accepted and respected the priests, but there were others who feared and resented their presence. No doubt certain leaders feared the loss of their leadership role, and thus were participants in groups who at various times murdered missionaries. Such an instance oc-curred in 1632, when two friars, Arvide and Letrado, were killed by Zunis, who then decamped to their traditional strong-hold atop Corn Mountain or Towayalane (also known as Thunder Mountain), a huge rock mesa about 1,000 feet above the valley floor some three miles from Zuni.

1630   The Dutch West India Company officials instructed: "The Pa-troons of New Netherland shall be found to purchase from the Lord Sachems (Indians) in New Netherland, the soil where they propose to plant their colonies, and shall acquire such right thereunto as they will agree with said Sachems."

1633   First land allotment policy was established by the General Court of the Massachusetts Colony.

1637   The Pequot War in New England erupted when the Pequot Indians, one of the few tribes not affected by the "plague," tried to resist invasions by settlers into the Connecticut Valley. Late one night a small party of whites surrounded the Indian settlement, set it afire, with the result that 500 were killed or burned to death. The remnants of this tribe were sold into slavery.

1640   The Assiniboin, a group of Indians sometimes called the Rocky Mountain Sioux, were discovered in the Dakotas by Jesuit priests and proved to be a distinct entity despite the virtual similarity of their language to that of the Sioux, historically their deadly enemies.

First mention of the Sioux in recorded history placed the tribe in an area west of the Great Lakes.

1641   The Dutch in New Amsterdam altered their original policy of offering rewards for heads to the policy of paying bounties for scalps.

1642   On February 25, Dutch settlers in New York repaid the Indian kindness by attacking them during the night, killing 120 men, women and children asleep in their wigwams. This was not the first "massacre," but it was a white massacre of Indians. Bayonettes were run through the stomachs of babies, who were then flung into the river. They cut off the hands of the men and cut open the women with their swords. They went among the Indians with fiery torches, burning homes until no Indians were left. These had been friendly Indians who had sold their Manhattan island for needles, awls and fish hooks. This attack was headed by Dutch Governor Kieft and Sergen Rudolf with a party of soldiers. (One historian has commented that this was probably the most atrocious brutaility existing in American Annals.)

1643   An Indian-English dictionary was published, entitled: A Key into the Language of America, or a help to the language of the natives in New England, together with brief observations of the customs, manners and workings of the aforesaid natives. (sic) Written by Roger Williams of Provincetown, prepared en route back to England, and published in London.

The original Indian-English dictionary was published.

1646   The English missionary, John Eliot, brought the Indians with whom he had been working into towns where he was able to improve his teaching in the art of township government and the ways of the white man. There is scanty evidence to sustain any claims that the Indian communities thus formulated ever entered into the "main stream" of the white colonial economic life.

The final attempt of Opechanough to eliminate the white man was crushed by Sir William Berkley's vigorous war of reprisal and removed the Indian threat to the point where they sued a peace which lasted for thirty years. Trouble flared up briefly in 1676-77, precipitating the Bacon Rebellion, but was quickly quelled.

1650 An ordinance was passed by the Director of Council of New Netherlands on May 30, attempting to remedy the counterfeiting of wampum (Indian shell money frequently used as necklaces, bracelets, belts, etc.). White traders had stooped to making imitations in Furope, thereby defrauding the unsophisticated Red man.

1660 The first Indian church in New England was founded by John Eliot in Natick, Massachusetts. By 1674 six other "praying" Indian towns had been established.

Metacomet, later renamed King Phillip by the colonists, assumed the role of chief of the Pequots. In Phillip the Indians had a stimulating, activist leader, one dedicated to driving the white man out of the country.

1661 The earliest translation of the Bible into an Indian (Algonquian) language was, "The Testament of Our Lord and Savior Jesus Christ," by John Eliot. It contained 130 pages and was written in the Algonquin Indian dialect. It was printed by the Commissioners of the United Colonies in New England for the "propagation of the Gospel of the Indians in New England" and was the first Bible to be printed in this country.

An Act by the State of Virginia authorized "silver and plated placques to be worn by Indians when they visited settlements." These were distributed only to friendly Indians and were an obvious early attempt to control movements.

1662 The Assembly, seated at James City, Virginia, enacted an ordinance "prohibiting the entertainment of Indians without badges (medals or placques)."

1663 In the French and Indian War, the Iroquois are felt by many historians to have been the ones who "tipped the balance of power." However, during the Revolutionary War they remained loyal to the English and caused the American Revolutionists many problems. In the post-revolutionary era, part of the Iroquois went to Canada to live, while another part remained in the United States. George Washington's just peace treaty (which offended some whites who vilified him for it), paid off during the War of 1812, when the Iroquois refused to join the Shawnee chief Tecumseh and thereby ended their ancient alliance with England.

1666   The Indian Grammar entitled in English "An Essay to Bring the Indian Language into Rules, for the Help of Such as Desire to Learn the Same, for the Furtherance of the Gospel Among Them," was written by John Eliot and printed in Cambridge by Normonduke Johnson. It was composed in the language of the Massachusetts Indians.

1670   Hiacoomes was ordained a Christian minister by John Eliot and John Cotten on August 22. He preached his first service to his own people at Martha's Vineyard, Massachusetts.

1672   October 7, a band of White Mountain Apaches raided Hawikun (the largest of the Zuni pueblos) and killed the friar, Pedro de Abila y Ayala.

1673   Pennsylvania State Archives reveal the first Indian transaction on February 8, "Tract of land on the Delaware Edward Cantwell and Johannes De Hous for:
    1 halfe ankar of drinke
    two match coates
    two axes, two barrs of lard
    four hand fulls of powder
    two knives, some paint
witnessed by Peter Jegou, Anth Bryant". (sic) Authorized and conveyed as 700 acres by Phillip Carterett, Governor of New Jersey.

1675   King Phillip (Metacomet), son of Chief Massasoit, gathered an estimated 20,000 other Indians who on June 24 led an attack in the southern part of New England, which started "King Phillip's War." The next year Phillip was slain. Hundreds of Indians, including his wife and nine year old son, were sold into captivity. His dream of unifying the various Indian tribes into a single unit to drive the white man back died with him. He had been perceptive enough to see the noose tightening around his

people, caught between the mighty Iroquois confederacy to his
west, and the expanding white colonists in front and circling his
flanks.

1676   Quanpen, an Indian chieftain (Sowagonish) was given a court
        martial on August 24 at Newport, by General Walter Case, and
        found guilty of having participated in King Phillip's War against
        the colonial people. He was ordered to be shot on August 26.

1680   It has been estimated that there were at least 2,500 Zuni in this
        year of the Pueblo Rebellion. Records quote the population in
        1860 at 1,580, with a gain of only another hundred noted in the
        1910 census. The increase has continued on a gradual curve
        with the 1941 census showing 2,252, the 1951 recording 2,922,
        and 1961 giving 4,213. Today's population is estimated at 5,100.

        The Great Pueblo Revolt occurred against the Spanish, who had
        virtually enslaved the Pueblo Indian. (The remains of a leg iron
        found on an Indian buried in "Old Town" Albuquerque, N.M.
        may be seen in the shop of Bricito Sewell - The Crazy Horse
        Trading Co.) This revolt was led by Pope of San Juan, Tupatu
        of the Picuris, Jaca and others, and brought twelve years of in-
        dependence from Spanish rule for the Rio Grande pueblos.
        Center of the revolt was the Taos pueblo and it was that pueblo
        that De Vargas attacked, causing the Indians to flee into the
        mountains and forests.

1682   Uncas, famous Mohegan chief, who was epitomized in James
        Fenimore Cooper's fiction book, The Last of the Mohicans, died
        in the State of Connecticut. Although he had married a Pequot
        chief's daughter, he had been banned by the Pequot, Narragansett,
        and their allies, against whom he subsequently warred with the
        white colonists. A memorial was later erected to his memory
        at Cooperstown, New York and Norwich, Connecticut.

        The Penn Treaty was signed with the Iroquois, and a letter was
        sent to their chief addressing him as the "Emperor of Canada."
        William Penn wrote his name on the great treaty which bears
        his name and which commenced a fifty year long period of peace.

1687   The Calmcoets (sometimes known as Karankawas) killed vir-
        tually the entire white party left by the French explorer at Fort
        St. Louis, located on the Lavaca River near Matagorda Bay on
        the Texas Gulf Coast.

1689   The Spanish Governor Cruzate, from position in exile outside of New Mexico where he had been driven during the Indian Pueblo Uprising Revolt in 1680, concluded that the Jemez Indians were repentant and is alleged to have made them an unasked-for grant of 17,000-plus acres in the Ojo del Espiritu Santo Grant.

1690   John Eliot, first missionary to the Indians of the New England area, died at the age of eighty-six years, after working diligently to educate and generally improve understanding of the Red man.

1691   The College of William and Mary was chartered in Virginia. In the following years, many Indian students were brought there for education.

1692   In January, Father Eusebio Francisco Kino, a Jesuit missionary who had been working to establish missions since 1687 amongst the Indians of Lower California, first visited the area of what is now Tumacacori National Monument, Arizona, near the border at Nogales, Mexico. He came at the invitation of the Sobaipuris Indians of San Xavier del Bac region who had heard about his work. With him was Father Juan Maria de Salvatierra. They conferred with the headmen, said Mass, and baptized some infants. The rancheria was a compact grouping of about forty homes built close together.

Santa Ana Pueblo was founded by the Padres about 12 miles northwest of Bernalillo, New Mexico. (The land near their pueblo is so sandy and full of alkalai that in the spring and summer the Indians used to leave the pueblo and live in the field along the Rio Grande at El Ranchito.)

1696   In the summer there was another uprising of the Indians, who resented the presence of the returned Spanish. It was short-lived and in the fall, DeVargas defeated the Indians and succeeded in establishing a permanent peace for the pueblos.

In the early summer, the Mohawk Indians of New York were punished by French Count Frontin, who led a sizeable invasion force and burned the Onondaga and Oneida castles to the ground, as well as destroying the cornfields surrounding the settlement.

1698   English Captain Walter Hyde observed the Five Nation Tribes of New York Indians and found that, "they generally live to the age of 80, 90 or 100 years without hardly a headache."

1701   Father Kino's expanding missionary efforts in Arizona resulted in four additional missionaries. One of these, Padre Juan de San Martin, was assigned a resident station of Guevavi, to which was added the rancheria of Tumacacori, as a vista. The stay was short-lived, and records do not mention it after a few years.

1703   The Apalachee Tribes of Florida were originally discovered by DeSoto and found to be a wealthy farming and industrious group famed for their fighting prowess. At first they sided with the Spanish, but suffered from raids instigated by the English government. In 1703 a group of white settlers and Indian allies swooped down on the Apalachee territory, burning missions and towns. In this expedition over 200 Apalachees were killed, and more than 1,400 taken back to be sold into slavery. The following year, another white raiding party completed the havoc by driving off the survivors to friendly tribes, in which their identity became extinct. Remembered by white men now only by such geographical designations as the Appalachian Mountains, Apalachee Bay in Florida and an assortment of counties and towns in Alabama, Florida and Georgia. Tallahassee, State capitol of Florida, comes from the Apalachian word meaning "Old Town."

1713   The Treaty of Utrect ceded Arcadia, New Foundland and the Hudson Bay Territory to England, and in addition noted that the Five Nations of Indians were British subjects, though this matter had not been discussed with the confederacy leaders.

1715   The Indian League of Nations was created, and the Tuscaroras joined.

          The Book of Common Prayers was printed in the Mohawk Indian language in New York City.

1717   Early American genocide was espoused by a prominent citizen of the South Carolina colony who said, "We must assist them in cutting one another's throats...This is the game we intend to play if possible...for if we cannot destroy one nation of Indians by another, our country will be lost."

Some time later, the policy of driving the Indians westward across the wide Missouri and Mississippi was adopted.

1720   The first permanent Indian school was created in Williamsburg, Virginia.

1722   English authorities in Massachusetts sent out an expedition to stop the activities of the Abnaki Indians, centered around the French mission operated by Father Rale at Norridgewock. In the fighting which ensued, the mission was destroyed, Father Rale was killed, and the Indians were defeated. Amongst the priest's papers was found an Abnaki dictionary which he is presumed to have created.

1723   The Brafferton Building, an imposing structure, was built on the College of William and Mary campus for Indian students, who attended in such numbers as to require such a gathering place. The building can be seen standing today.

1725   On February 25, a party of New Hampshire militia volunteers came across a group of sleeping Indians and scalped all of them. Later they collected from the city of Dover a bounty of one hundred pounds, paid from public funds, for each scalp.

1730   On September 30, seven Cherokee chiefs and headmen visited the British Court at London and entered into the alliance known as "The Articles of Agreement" with the Lords Commissioners. This was the outcome of negotiations started at Nequassee, now Georgia, on April 3, at which Sir Alexander Cumings convinced the Indians to accept Montoy as "Emperor."

1733   Tomochichi, noted Creek chief, outlawed by his people, became friendly with the founders of the Georgia Colony and assisted in a treaty of alliance between the lower Creek Indians and whites.

1734   Lord Oglethorpe, founder of the Georgia colony, presented Chief Tomochichi of the Creeks and other Indians to the Trustees and Lords of the Georgia Colony during a meeting in London. (Note: a photograph of that may be viewed in the Smithsonian Institute.)

1738   Small pox was brought by white slave traders to Charlestown, South Carolina, and from there conveyed to the Cherokees in

Georgia, in goods sold to the Indians. The disease killed almost half of the tribe.

1744   King George's War was the alleged reason for a rupture of the status quo in the new American region. The French fought the British, aided by their Indian allies, until 1748, when the Treaty of Aix-la Chapelle quieted things for a time, restoring the territories which had been seized by one side to the former tenant.

1751   Benjamin Franklin, writing about his proposed Albany Plan of Union for the American colonists, paid a high tribute to the Iroquois Confederation's development of their confederated government system. In a March 20 letter to Mr. Parker he wrote: "It would be a very strange thing, if Six Nations of ignorant savages should be capable of forming a scheme for such a union, and be able to execute it in such a manner, as that it appears indissoluble; and yet that a like union should be impracticable for ten or a dozen English colonies, to whom it is more necessary and must be more advantageous, and who cannot be supposed to want an equal understanding of their interest."

1752   As a result of the Pima Indian rebellion against the Spaniards and the padres in November of 1751, Governor Parrilla of Sonora decided to establish a presidio in Tubac, three miles north of Tumacacori, Arizona. To keep the Spanish influence alive, he ordered a garrison of 50 soldiers to keep order in this vast area.

1754   The Albany Congress of English Colonies met to discuss a united colonial Indian policy.

1755   Edmund Atkin, English Agent for Southern Indian Tribes, reported to the Board of Trade: "No people in the world understand and pursue their true national interests better than the Indians. How sanguinary so ever they are towards their enemies, from a misguided passion of heroism, and a love for their country, yet they are in other ways truly human, hospitable and equitable...In their public treaties, no people are more open, explicit, and direct, nor are they excelled by any in the observance of them."

The English proclaimed that each Indian scalp would be worth 40 English pounds. One research has observed that by the time the scalps were redeemed for bounties, it was difficult to say if they belonged to friend or foe.

1758   The first state Indian reservation was established on August 29,
        when New Jersey legislators appropriated 1,600 acres of Indian
        mills to be used as a reservation for Indians of that state. Called
        Brotherton, about 200 Indians, possibly Lenapes and Unamis,
        located upon it until it was sold about 1801.

1762   Austenaco, one of the principal chiefs of the Cherokees, was a
        member of a party who had portraits painted while in London.
        Stalking Turkey, also a chief, was another delegate. The En-
        glishmen of that day were supposed to be very colorful in their
        dress, but the visiting Indians made a tremendous impression
        as they walked the streets of London. (These portraits may be
        viewed in the Smithsonian Institute.)

1763   King George III's policy towards the Indians was made known
        in a proclamation which set aside "reserved lands" for Indians.

        Pontiac attacked Detroit in May and started a short-lived war
        which saw fort after fort fall before Indian onslaught. Lord
        Jeffrey Amherst is alleged to have uttered an idea for an early
        attempt at biological warfare, by infecting Indians with small-
        pox. He did insist, 'I need only add, that I wish to hear of no
        prisoners, should any of the villains be met with arms.''

1764   The English Plan for an Imperial Department of Indian Affairs
        was announced.

1765   An Indian preacher, Samson Occum, visited England and raised
        money to help support the activities of Dartmouth College, which
        had been established in 1750 as a school for Indians.

1767   A Spanish royal decree, attributable to a feud between the men
        of the cloth and the military, ordered the Jesuits out of New
        Spain. King Carlos III felt that continued presence of the Jesuits
        was not in the best interests of the crown. The complete and
        detailed story of the rivalry, the personalities and the methods
        used by both groups would take many pages to explain, and the
        reader is referred elsewhere for that story.

1768   The earliest civil grant recorded in the United States was the
        Watauga Commonwealth and the Independent Civil Government,
        established by the Treaty of Fort Stanwick. The Six Nations

agreed to surrender all the lands between the Ohio and the Tennessee rivers to the English. Apparently there was some misunderstanding, because the Iroquois had ceded land to which they had no legal right. The settlers organized a civil government in May 1772, with the "Articles of the Watauga Association" as a basis for existence. This was the first free and independent community established in the American continent.

1769   Franciscan missionaries urged the Indians of California to accept the Christian religion and settle about the missions, around which they often constructed irrigation networks. The Indians were taught cattle raising and various crafts to help make their life more tolerable.

1770   The Yokuts Indians of the San Joaquin Valley in California were judged to have a population of approximately 18,000, of which a mere handful remain in that western state today.

1775   One of the early Acts of the Continental Congress, on July 12, 1775 was to declare its control over Indian tribes by creating three departments of Indian Affairs: a Northern, a Southern and a Middle Department, with Commissioners at the head of each who were charged with duties comparable to those of men who later headed the post of Superintendent. An indication of the importance Congress gave to the matter was in the naming of such luminaries as Benjamin Franklin, Patrick Henry and James Wilson to these departments.

On July 12, the Continental Congress appropriated $500 for the education of Indian youth at Dartmouth College, New Hampshire. This was increased to $5,000 five years later.

The newly appointed Colonial Indian Commissioners opened the first negotiations with Indian groups (Six Nations) in July. An interesting provision required the employment of two blacksmiths among the Indians and the opening of trade.

1776   Sometime about May 24 Don Felipe Velderrain, the alferez of Tubac, Arizona, visited Father Font at Caborca to advise that nothing remained at the mission station at Tumacacori, for the place had been sacked by Apaches while the garrison was away. The Apaches managed to get very valuable horses and cattle and caused considerable damage.

1777   Defeated by whites, in an attempt to reduce encroachments in East Tennessee Valley, Chief Dragger Canoe and the Cherokees were forced to sign treaties ceding away large tracts of land.

1778   The Delaware Tribes were offered the prospect of statehood in a negotiated treaty. Actual admittance of an Indian state to the union of thirteen states was never made, for reasons unclear at this late date. The treaty with the Delawares on September 17 was the first of 370 which were to be concluded with Indians.

George Washington wrote on March 13 from Valley Forge to the Commissioners of Indian Affairs: "...I am empowered to employ a body of four hundred Indians, if they can be procured upon proper terms...I think they may be made of excellent use, as scouts and light troops, mixed with our own parties."

During the terrible winter at Valley Forge, Dr. Waldo, a surgeon, wrote: "...I was called to relieve a soldier thought to be dying. He expired before I reached the hut. He was an Indian, an excellent soldier, and has fought for the very people who disinherited his forefathers."

A Treaty of Peace with the Delawares on September 17, at what is now Pittsburgh, provided that all offenses be immediately mutually forgiven, that peace and friendship be perpetually maintained, and that in the case of war there would be mutual assistance. The U.S. was to have free passage to the forts and towns of their former enemies, and such men as could be spared were to join the colonial armies. Neither was to inflict punishment without an impartial trial. All territorial rights were to be respected which had been granted by former treaties, and a representative of the Indians would be permitted in Congress under certain conditions.

September 17 witnessed the conclusion of the first treaty between the United States government and an Indian tribe, the Delaware Indians. Until the Civil War era, governmental policy in dealing with the Indian tribes was based on a treaty, with the Tribes considered as independent nations. However, during and after the War Between the States, this attitude was supplanted by one that treated the Indians as objects of national charity having no legal rights. In 1862, the Secretary of the

Interior wrote that the tribes had none of the elements of na-
tionality, and that they resided within an area under the control
of the United States. Continuing in this vein, he said, "the
rapid progress of civilization upon this continent will not permit
the lands which are required for cultivation to be surrendered
to save tribes for hunting grounds. Further, indeed, whatever
may be the theory, the Government has always demanded the
removal of the Indians when their lands were required for agricultural purposes by advancing settlements. Although the consent of the Indians has been obtained in the form of treaties, it
is well known that they have yielded to a necessity to which they
could not resist. A radical change in the mode of treatment
of Indians should, in my judgment, be adopted. Instead of being
treated as independent nations, they should be regarded as wards
of the government, entitled to its fostering care and protection.
Suitable districts should supply them, through its own Agents,
with such articles as they use, until they can be instructed to
earn their subsistence by their labor."

1779   General John Sullivan of Washington's army inadvertently destroyed a most advanced society during a campaign against hostile
Iroquois. Numerous brick and stone houses were destroyed,
hundreds of acres of vegetables and fruit were ruined, and orch-
ards were cut down, or the trees ringed.

1782   Christian Delaware Indians were massacred at Gnanenhutten,
Ohio. Upon the advice of the English, to avoid conflicts with
white farmers, the Indians voluntarily moved away to Sandusky,
Since they had already planted the fields in the old place, however, it was necessary for some members to return to harvest
the life-saving food. There they were discovered by a band of
one hundred white men under Colonel David Williamson. The
white group promptly took away the Indian arms, tied them up,
and then with the Indians' own hand weapons killed them, thereby conserving ammunition. It is recorded that the Red men
prayed and sang hymns while thirty-five men, twenty-seven
women and thirty-four children were inhumanly killed.

1783   Congress issued a proclamation warning against buying or
"squatting on" Indian lands.

1784   "Forced removal" of Indian tribes began.

The Russians established the first school in Alaska at Three Saints Bay, Kodiak Island.

Congress ordered the War Office to provide militia troops to assist the Indian Commissioners who were negotiating Indian treaties.

1786   The first <u>Federal</u> Indian reservation was established. On August 7, the Confederation Congress established two departments: the Northern with jurisdiction north of the Ohio River and west of the Hudson River (in New York); and the Southern, which covered south of the Ohio River. A superintendent at the head of each reported to the Secretary of War. Each of these officials had the power to grant licenses to trade and live with the Indians.

1787   The Northwest Ordinance was prominent in creating the basis for settlement of whites beyond the Alleghenies and in the formulation of Indian policy. It states: "The utmost of good faith shall always be observed toward the Indians; their land and property shall never be taken away from them without their consent; and their property, rights and liberty shall never be invaded by Congress; but laws founded in justice and humanity shall from time to time be made for preventing wrongs to them, and for preserving peace and friendship with them." The Northwest Ordinance refers to what is now a large part of the "Middle West."

1789   Henry Knox, the first Secretary of War and Indian Administration, observed, "The civilization of the Indian will require the highest knowledge of human character, and a steady perserverance in a wise supervision over a service of years."

On August 7, the War Department was established by Congress, with Indian Affairs remaining a function of the Secretary of War. That first Congress and President Washington observed the need for remedying the serious problem created by the conflict between Indian and White interests. Congressional policy was set forth in Article 3 of the Act of August 7, 1789, to the effect that "The utmost good faith shall always be observed towards the Indians; their land and their property shall never be taken from them without their consent and their property, rights and liberty shall never be invaded or disturbed, unless in just and lawful wars authorized by Congress, but laws founded in justice and humanity shall from time to time be made, for preventing wrongs being done to them, and for preserving peace and friendship with them."

Congress authorized territorial governors as ex-officio Indian Superintendents under the guidance of the War Department.

The Congress appropriated $20,000 for the purpose of negotiating and trading with the Indian tribes.

1790   The Miami Expedition composed of 400 state militia troops under the command of Colonel John Hardin, retreated in defeat from battle with the Indians in the Northwestern Ohio territory. This was the initial battle fought by U.S. troops after the formation of the U.S.A. (The white men lost this battle due to ineptness, lack of training, poor guns, and inadequate leadership.)

Congress passed an Act for the purpose of regulating trade and intercourse with Indian tribes. The latter provided for licensing Indian traders and gave vast regulatory powers to the President. (During the period 1796-1822 many trading houses were maintained under government ownership for the purpose of offering a "fair price" for Indian furs in exchange. The Agents in charge of the trading houses were appointed by the President and were responsible to him.)

1791   The Senecas wrote to General Washington imploring him to give them teachers so that their men might be taught to farm and build houses, their squaws to spin and weave, and their children to read and write.

In October, the white man suffered his worst defeat in history from the Red man and quite probably the worst in all of the Indian wars, when Little Turtle attacked General Arthur St. Clair, Governor of the Northwest Territory, and some 1,400 untrained militia on the Wabash River. St. Clair's casualties of 900 (630 killed) made Custer's later loss of 211 at the Little Big Horn seem small in comparison. Actually, even Braddock lost fewer men who were killed in action - 725 out of a command of 1,200 men.

1793   Congress, in the Second Intercourse Act, authorized an expenditure of not more than $20,000 annually for the purchase of domestic animals and farming implements for the Indian nations.

(It proved to be an insufficient sum to be effective, despite President Washington's advice to the Indians to stop warring and adopt the white men's ways.) It also provided for Presidential appointment of temporary Agents among the Indian tribes.

1794   The first Indian treaty was signed agreeing to provide education for the Oneidas, Tuscaroras and Stockbridges. This first treaty, which specifically mentioned education, provided that teachers would be employed to "instruct some young men of these three nations in the arts of the miller and the sawer."

1795   The American Government "factory" system was introduced in the states to counteract the influence of English and Spanish settlers.

1796   The era of horseback cultivation and culture of the High Plains Indians began. These Indians had gradually discarded canoes and dogs to haul their goods as they were able to get horses in increasing numbers from traders and contacts with the Indians from Northern tribes. (Considered by a number of writers to be a convenient date for this beginning.)

Government policy was formulated making lawful the Indian trading Houses which were to be operated by the government as an attempt to diminish the influence of the British, French and Spanish on the frontier.

Benjamin Hawkins, appointed by President Washington as Creek Agent and Superintendent of Southern Indians, while working a part of the "factory system" developed a life-time interest in the problems of the Indians. He devoted his life to solution and eradication of the difficulties.

1799   Handsome Lake, a reformed Iroquois alcoholic, arose as a prophet for his frustrated people after the Revolution and preached that the old Iroquois had a good but incomplete life because they lacked full understanding of God. A cult sprang up around him as he preached reaction to the old tribal ways and rejection of white customs, including the use of ploughs.

Early   The Karankawa Indians fought a valiant but desperate battle with
1800's the New Orleans pirate, Jean Lafitte, because he stole one of their tribeswomen. The vain-glorious effort was doomed, because the Indians lacked the firearms possessed by Lafitte's men.

1801   Napoleon sold Louisiana to the United States, thereby paving the way for the American government to explore the new lands which doubled the territory and were unknown except to a scattered handful of whites.

1802   The government passed a law forbidding liquor sales to Indians in compliance with a request from two trading posts which competed with the Spanish for Creek and Cherokee business.

1803   The second mention of education in a treaty occurred when the government included a proviso to pay $100 a year for seven years towards the support of a priest who was to "instruct as many children as possible in the rudiments of literature."

1804   In May, Lewis and Clark set out from St. Louis on a mission from President Jefferson to explore and map the new Louisiana Purchase territory. Their JOURNALS contain a careful description of the wild life and peoples noticed. The winter of 1804-1805 was spent in North Dakota with the Mandan Indians. Their initial good fortune turned against Lewis and Clark in September, 1805. They almost starved and were reduced to eating their pack horses and munching on roots as they clambered their way over the Rockies. Vital agreements with the Shoshones were made to obtain replacement horses.

1806   The Office of Superintendent of Indian Trade was established. The duties of this newly appointed bureau included the purchase and charge of all goods intended for trade with the Indian nations.

1807   Fray Narciso Guitierrez successfully petitioned the intendente of the province, via Juan Legarra, governor of the pueblo of Tumacacori, to issue new title papers covering some 52,000 acres of land, of what was to be known as the Tumacacori Land Grant, Arizona, for farming and ranching purposes. All of this was to support a new church built the year before.

1808   The Indian Princess, an operatic melodrama, was the original play about an Indian, written by James Nelson Barber and produced on April 6 at the Chestnut Theatre in Philadelphia.

1809   By terms of the Treaty of Fort Wayne, General William Henry Harrison (Governor of the Territory of Indiana 1800-1812), obtained 2,500,000 acres of land from the Indians.

Sequoya, a Cherokee without formal education or knowledge of English, pledged himself to providing a written language for the Indians. He became so engrossed with his mission that he removed himself from the main village in order to work without interruption. Fellow tribesmen scorned his efforts at first; then their feelings changed to fear. Feeling that he was involved with witchcraft, they burned his cabin and all of his records, studies and investigations. Undaunted, he re-did his work, which was interrupted only by tribal requirements to travel and to serve in the Cherokee army. Miraculously, he was able to devise an alphabet which systematized the Cherokee language into eighty-five different sounds, and provided a symbol for each. Twelve hard years bore fruit!

A Treaty with the Delaware, Potawatomies, Miamis, Kickapoos and Eel River tribes gave the U.S. government three million acres of choice land along the Wabash River for a mere $8,200 cash.

1810   Many bands of Indians met at what are now the Rosebud and Standing Rock agencies in South Dakota.

1812   The Oglala Sioux tribe of South Dakota conducted their first hunt for wild horses, which they roped and kept for their own.

1814   The End of the War of 1812 finished the possibilities of alliance between European countries and Indian Tribes.

In July, General Andrew Jackson turned on his friends of the War of 1812, the Cherokees and the Creeks, demanding and receiving 23 million acres of Creek land, estimated to be 3/5 of Alabama and 1/5 of Georgia.

1815-   A number of post-War of 1812 treaties, which attempted to re-
1825   solve matters of trading areas and initiated the removal of the red man to new western lands, were concluded with Indian tribes living north of the Ohio River.

1817   In his first annual message to Congress, President James Monroe said, "...The earth was given to mankind to support the greatest numbers of which it is capable, and no tribe, or people have a right to withhold from the wants of others more than is necessary for their own support and comfort...." Such a philosophy gave support to the land grabbers and to advocates of forcible removal of Indians from their own land .

1819   Floridian boundaries were finally resolved with England, thereby bringing more Indian lands into federal policy discussions .

Congress set up a program for the civilization of the Indians, called the Civilization Fund . (Again, it was to be too small an amount to accomplish anything useful; only a mere $10,000 annually .) These funds were distributed among the various mission groups, presumably enabling them to widen their educational programs .

1820   Jedidiah Morse, appointed by President Monroe to survey Indian removal problems and to furnish the Secretary of War, John Calhoun, with a report, wrote: "To remove these Indians from their homes ...into a wilderness among strangers, possibly hostile, to live as their neighbors live, by hunting, a state to which they have not been lately accustomed, and which is incompatible with civilization, can hardly be reconciled with the professed object of civilizing them ."

1821   Mexico declared its independence from Spain, and thereby ushered in a new set of overlords for the Indians in what is now parts of California, Arizona and New Mexico .

1822   Congress abolished the system of Indian trading houses and the Office of Indian Affairs .

David Moncock of the Creek Tribe of the territory of Alabama was graduated from the United States Military Academy, after having been the first Indian to be admitted (and the only one to graduate from that institution). He became a Major and, ironically, was killed in the Creek War of 1836.

The Office of Superintendent of Indian Affairs, located at St. Louis, Missouri, was created for western lands .

1823   Sequoya, a Cherokee of mixed blood, presented his tribe with a formulated and written alphabet. This represented the first, and one of the few formal breaks, with the practice of not writing before the coming of the white man, although pictographs had appeared on rocks and in caves. (One of the best known and most famous ritual records, believed to have been originally recorded in pictographs cut upon wood, is the Walam Olum of the Delawares.) Nothing above the level of the simplest picture writing (best developed by the Indians around the Great Lakes region, where birchbark instead of paper was used) had been devised until Sequoya's achievement.

Supreme Court Justice John Marshall rendered a court opinion which seemed to approve the prevailing method of gaining title to the lands of the Indians involved. "...these grants have been understood by all to convey a title to grantees, subject only to the Indian right of occupancy." (Emphasis supplied.) It likewise evolved and permitted ex post facto assurances that the Indians could not be denied "due process." More than one hundred years later, we can see that this turned out to be a protective device for the Indians. In commenting on the Indians' winning of the case, President Jackson said, "John Marshall has made his decision; let him embrace it." The Removal Act of 1830 soon followed, showing Jackson's mood.

1825   A census taken among the Cherokee tribe in Georgia revealed that they possessed 33 grist mills, 13 sawmills, one powder mill, 69 blacksmith shops, two tab yards, 762 looms, 2486 spinning wheels, 172 wagons, 2923 plows, 7683 horses, 22,531 black cattle, 46,732 swine and 2566 sheep. This tabulation tends to refute the claims of some that all Indians were mere primitive hunters and prosaic peoples, rather than hard-working tillers of the soil and educated peoples that Cherokees and others of the "Five Civilized Tribes" were, in fact. It would likewise tend to refute allegations at that time that Indians would not be harmed by removing them from their lands, which subsequently occurred.

1825-   The period of the growth and development of the famed Choc-
1842   taw Academy. This institution, located in the present-day Georgetown, Kentucky countryside, was the dream of the Indians who worked to see their dream fulfilled. It was supported by them for the purpose of providing their children with training in the ways of the white man.

1826   Elias Boudinot, a full-blooded Cherokee, reported to a meeting of the First Presbyterian Church in Philadelphia on the progress of his people through missionary aid: "It is a matter of surprise to me, and must be to all who are properly acquainted with the conditions of the aborigines of the country, that the Cherokees have advanced."

1827   The Indians adopted the Cherokee Constitution, but shortly there-after it was nullified by the legislature of the State of Georgia.

1828   The Cherokee Phoenix, a weekly newspaper printed in both English and Cherokee was published on February 21, and re-mained in business until October 1835, at New Echota, Georgia. The editor was Elias Boudinot, a Cherokee who had been edu-cated at a foreign mission school in Cornwall, Connecticut by a philanthropist whose name he adopted.

1829   The Cherokee Temperance Society was organized at New Echota, Georgia.

The first edition of the Cherokee Hymn Book was printed at New Echota, Georgia. Included in that original book were old Chris-tian and Cherokee hymns which had been handed down through oral tradition.

The Cass-Clark Report in regularizing Federal Indian adminis-tration was made known.

1830   President Jackson in an Act of May 28 provided for removal of Indians from lands upon which they had lived and hunted, but which were now desired by white settlers.

1832   U.S. Indian Affairs Commissioner Elbert Herring was appointed by President Jackson July 10, in accordance with an Act of July 9 to the post of Commissioner of Indian Affairs. (4 Stat L564) He had "direction and management of all matters arising out of Indian relations."

In the Treaty of Paynes Landing, executed under President Jack-son's order, the interpreter deliberately falsified the transla-tion of the treaty with the Seminoles.

Governmental health services for Indians began when Congress authorized funds to provide for smallpox vaccination of a num-ber of tribes.

"America was inhabited by a distinct people, divided into separate nations, independent of each other, and of the rest of the world, and governing themselves by their own laws," stated U.S. Supreme Court Chief Justice John Marshall in Worcester v. Georgia (6 Peters 515).

1832-   By various devices - force, fraud, deception, persuasion, etc.,
1839   the Indians of the Five Civilized Tribes were driven out of their home grounds and removed to Oklahoma. There are many accounts of the bribing of several chiefs who signed away the old lands and forced exile, beginning with the trek called "The Trail of Tears." En route some of the Indians were shot and bayonetted because they were too slow in moving to please their military escorts.

1834   The Indian Trade and Intercourse Act was passed on June 30 and signed by President Jackson.

By this date there were estimated to be 30,000 Indians living at California missions. Indians of that state believe that the misconception that the padres "encouraged" Indians to live in that state started with the early history textbooks and has erroneously persisted. Many Indian leaders point out that Roman Catholic church history can attest to the fact that certain mission priests considered it their duty to bring the Indians under the control of the church. Some were very cruel and inhuman in their use of leg irons, wrist irons and other means of gaining submission.

The Indian Act of this year required the white man to pay a toll for each head of cattle which passed over the red man's land. (The Indians of the Five Civilized Tribes had their own herds, rich grazing land, and thereby had become relatively wealthy.)

1835   The Cherokee Phoenix newspaper was denied the Freedom of the Press guaranteed by the first amendment of the U.S. Constitution when it incurred the displeasure of the Georgia governor, who solicited the help of the state militia in closing down this newspaper.

On May 12 the Mexican Government authorized the selection of available vacant lands in Texas for "peaceable and civilized Indians which may have been introduced into Texas."

Sam Houston, John Forbes and John Cameron, were appointed Indian Commissioners by the Ex-officio President of the Grand Council of the Provisional Government of Texas on December 22. The action was ratified on December 28 by Governor Henry Smith.

1836   Despite deplorable treatment at the hands of the white settlers, which over a period of thirteen years resulted in the loss of about half their population, the Karankawa Indians fought with the Americans in the Texas War for Independence. In that war they paid a heavy price with the loss of their chief and many warriors.

1835-   This was the period of the Seminole War.
1842

1837   The President signed the Act of January 9, which regulated the disposition of ceded Indian lands.

The western smallpox epidemic of that year was terrible in the intensity with which it hit many Indian tribes. This plague decimated the powerful Mandan and Hidatso, killing 1450 of a total Mandan population of 1600, while the Hidatso fared a proportionate fate. Today these two, coupled with the Archare tribe, are located in Montana, and while their numbers have increased, they are still a mere twenty percent of their former numbers.

1838   In the Spring, 7,000 federal troops were sent to complete the removal of the Cherokees from the state of Georgia. Their leaders, who had vigorously opposed the treaty removal - even to the U.S. Supreme Court and the President in Washington - saw their people forcibly taken from their homes and fields and placed in stockades pending their departure. It is pertinent to note that fear and despondency, added to disease and exposure, exacted a great toll on the Indians, for about twenty-five percent never reached the proposed new lands. The Cherokees remember the trek as "The Trail Where They Cried," while the white historians call it "The Trail of Tears." Thereafter the U.S. Indian Removal Policy, as such, ended, but the philosophy is still prevalent in governmental thinking.

1840's   Indian control changed with the transfer of their jurisdiction from the War Department to the Department of the Interior.

Era of paternalism - assimilation - break-up of reservations and allocation of lands to individual members of a tribe.

1841   The white people at Norwich, Connecticut, impressed by Indian reverence for a dead Narranganset Chief, erected the first monument by whites to an Indian at "Sachem's Plains".

1842   Henry E. Scott was appointed Indian Commissioner of the Republic of Texas by President Sam Houston on July 25.

There were 37 Indian schools reported to be in operation.

1843   The Russian-Greek Orthodox Church established the first mission school for Eskimos in Nushagak, Alaska.

The Nez Perces were described in the Report of the Indian Commissioner as "noble, industrious, sensible."

During an important tribal council meeting at Tahlequah, Oklahoma, Cherokee members made wampum belts which depicted the peace they had concluded with the Iroquois before the Revolutionary War. The Iroquois tribe prizes these old record belts, and some may be viewed at the New York State Historical Society's museum located in Albany, New York.

The Cherokee Temperance Society's Constitution was published soon after their forced removal from Georgia to Oklahoma.

1845-   War between the United States and Mexico.
1848

1846   With the Annexation of Texas, additional Indian tribes were added to U.S. governmental control and administration.

1847   A monument was erected by the citizens of Norwich, Connecticut, to the memory of Uncas, famous Mohegan chief, memorialized in the book of fiction written by James Fenimore Cooper, The Last of the Mohicans. Uncas in reality was a true and important friend of the whites in their problems with the Pequot, Narranganset and allied Indian tribes.

1848   The transfer of land to the United States by Mexico, under the terms of the Treaty of Guadalupe Hidalgo, added more Indian tribes. The American government promised to adhere to the rights and treaties honored by the Mexicans.

A report stated that there were 87 boarding schools and sixteen manual arts training schools being operated for Indians.

1849   Congress acted to transfer the Bureau of Indian Affairs from the War Department to the newly created Interior Department.

The discovery of gold in the state of California added to the misery of the "mission" Indians, who were already suffering from the withdrawal of support and direction of the Spanish priests, who had, unfortunately, made them a dependent people. When Old Mexico became independent of Spain, the missions lost financial support from Europe and were forced to shut down, with consequent devastating effects on the Indians, who had lost self-sufficiency under mission direction. In their gold fever, the whites violently thrust aside the demoralized Indian in their attempt to get the valuable mineral. Initially, a number of treaties were signed to provide the red men with reservations in exchange for their land rights, but white politicians from the new state of California prevented the agreements from receiving ratification. As a consequence, the Indian groups wandered about, having surrendered possession of their own lands and not having any replacements on which to settle. Ultimately some meager and unsatisfactory adjustments were made, so that today there are more than 100 reservations in California, some that cover as much as 25,000 acres but others as ridiculously small as two acres. Actual compensation for the taking of the lands by the whites is still unsettled!

1850's   Federal agents obtained concessions from the Indian tribes, who were promised that reservations would be established. However, the U.S. Senate refused to ratify most of the agreements. It was not until 1944 that the government acknowledged their poor handling of Indian claims and rights, and paid more than $5 million compensation to Indian descendents.

1851   By the Treaty of Fort Laramie, the Plains Indians defined their territories and promised to stop hostile acts in return for which they were promised annuities by governmental agents. Unfortunately, the U.S. Senate cut down the lengths of the annuities and ruined the effect of the document. Eventually the states of Colorado, Kansas, South Dakota, North Dakota, Montana, Nebraska and Wyoming were carved from ceded land.

1852   Bloomfield School in Oklahoma, the first missionary school for Chickasaw girls, was opened.

The Town Council of Wolftown, North Carolina, dictated that the borrowers from the money-lending Cherokee tribe would have to pay interest at the rate of twenty percent for four month's use of the capital.

The Chilkats sent a mounted force over three hundred miles to destroy a Hudson Bay Company's trading post when that operation interfered with their monopoly of trade with Indians of that region. It is noteworthy that the Chilkats did not harm the trading post's captured inhabitants, but turned them loose with a stern warning of harsher fate if they returned to resume trading in the Indian domain. Tribes from the northern region of the state pf Washington tended to be warlike. They had resisted Russian attempts in 1799 to establish forts in Tlingit territory near Sitka, and burned the Europeans out. Others fared similar fates through the years.

1853   The Gadsden Purchase from Mexico resulted in the acquisition of more Indians and their lands in the states now known as Arizona, New Mexico and California.

Kit Carson was appointed Indian Agent at Taos, New Mexico. His home there is a museum open to the public today.

In a much-publicized battle, a force of about 100 Sac-Fox Indians, who had only shortly before been removed to Kansas, had a stand-off battle with 1,000 Plains Indians, who had vowed to destroy buffalo hunters coming from the East.

1854   Indian Commissioner George Manypenny pleaded for the abandonment of the Removal Policy, saying: "By alternate persuasion and force, some of these tribes have been removed, step by step, from mountains to valley, and from river to plain, until they have been pushed half-way across the continent. They can go no further. On the ground they now occupy, the crises must be met, and their future determined."

Preference in employment in the Indian Bureau is granted to those applicants who have one-quarter or more Indian blood, where two or more candidates are qualified for a new appointment to a particular vacancy. Today more than half of the BIA's employees are of Indian ancestry.

1856   Indian Commissioner George Manypenny wrote, "In no former equal period of our history have so many treaties been made, or such vast accession of land obtained." (Through fifty-two different treaties from 1853 to 1857 a total of 157 million acres of Indian land were acquired by the United States government.)

1858   U.S. Court of Claims Case Book D-546 reveals "United States agrees to purchase from Yanktown Sioux (South Dakota) the transfer of the Pipestone Quarry, 11 million acres of land (worth approximately $13,750,000 by its own valuation experts) for the sum of $1,650,000." Thus they made an immediate profit of $12,100,000.

1859   Executive Order of the United States set aside the first lands for the Indians of the United States in Arizona. Today, the estimated Indian population of that state is over 100,000, and their recognized land area comprises 16,034,802 acres.

1860   The second mission school was established for Indians of Alaska at Kwikpak.

The Yakima Agency Boarding School opened in November, with twenty-five Indian pupils in residence. This original boarding school was provided and promised under Article 5 of the Treaty with the Yakima Nation of June 5, 1855. (12 Stat L951) .

1860-   U.S. Army units under the command of Col. E.R.S. Canby,
1861   used the heliograph, a system of mirrors, for communications between detachments in their campaigns against the Navajos in New Mexico, thus establishing the U.S. Signal Corps.

1861   Southern promises during the War between the States caused
1865   some Indians to hope for return of old Indian lands. Indian fought Indian as sides were drawn up, with a few tribes remaining neutral and aloof.

1861   In March, the Confederate government organized a Bureau of Indian Affairs and appointed General Albert Pike of Arkansas to head its activities.

Stand Watie, a Cherokee, became the only Indian Brigadier-General in the Confederate Army. He commanded two Cherokee regiments fighting in the Southwest.

Union troops were no longer available to guard the reservations, which were split in their sympathies for the opposing forces during the War between the States. To escape involvement in the War, five thousand Creeks of Oklahoma under Chief Opothle, Union sympathizers, started an eastward trek towards Kansas. They were joined by 1500 Seminoles under their leader, Tustenuggee. They were attacked by white forces who were beaten off. A second time a combined white and Cherokee force came upon them, but the Cherokees refused to attack their fellow red men and left, declaring they had enlisted to fight white men and not Indians. Ultimately, though, the Union sympathizers were slaughtered in running battles with white Confederate cavalrymen, and only a few survived to tell the tale in Kansas at a tiny settlement.

1862   By May, Confederate Indian troops from Indian territories numbered 6435 men. The Cherokees, fighting for the Confederacy in the Thomas Legion, were purposely utilized in hunting down deserters, enemy scouts, bushwhackers and bands of Union sympathizers who had holed-up in the mountains of the Carolinas, Tennessee, etc.

The Minnesota Sioux Uprising of this year was noted later, in the Peace Commissioners' Report of 1867, to have been caused by Indian agents' corruption or incompetence.

Caleb Smith, Secretary of the Interior Department, proposed a "radical change in the mode of treatment of Indians" to look at them as "wards" of the government. Thus the work of the Bureau of Indian Affairs was often in opposition to military policy, and many times it acted as a restless and unfortunate buffer between the Indians and the U.S. Army.

1863   The Pinole Treaty of Tontobasin was arranged at Bloody Tanks (now Miami, Arizona). Through the ruse of a peace conference,

white settlers poisoned twenty-four Apaches. (It is worthy to
note that gold had recently been found in nearby Prescott!)

1863-   The hated Indian fighter, Kit Carson, led Southwestern cam-
1864   paigns against the Navajos and the Apaches.

1864   The Sand Creek Massacre of Cheyenne and Arapahos on Novem-
         ber 29, by troops led by Colonel John M. Chivington, led to
         public outcries against such needless brutalities. It became
         one of the bloodiest dates of the Civil War years. The Indians
         had come from Kansas and Colorado to confer, and had been
         ordered to camp at a site on Sand Creek, where they were
         treacherously attacked by the whites without provocation.

         The March of Tears, made by 8000 Indians from Navajoland to
         the Bosque Redondo (Fort Sumner, N.M.), was led by Colonel
         Kit Carson. Here the Navajos were held in captivity under
         miserable conditions until 1868.

1866   On August 1, U.S. Indian Scouts were established within the
         Army by order of the War Department to provide "in the terri-
         tories and Indian country a force of Indians not to exceed one
         thousand, to act as scouts, who shall receive the pay and al-
         lowances of cavalry soldiers." In the next year they reached
         474, and within ten years the figure had risen to 600.

         The Fetterman Massacre took place on the Bozeman Trail on
         December 21.

1867   The Board of Indian Commissioners was established by the Pres-
         ident to consider the problems of the red man. Grant's action
         resulted from public disclosures of fraud and wrongdoing in
         his administration.

         The Peace Commission blamed white men for many of the troubles
         with the Plains Indians.

         The Cherokee National Council passed a law requiring white
         cattlemen to pay ten cents for each head of cattle passing on
         Indian lands, as permitted by the Act of 1834. Recognizing that
         they would be hurt by unregulated grazing of white man's cattle,
         and desiring to avoid barren ground, other tribes followed suit
         and erected toll gates for collection. Thus they followed the
         practice of law and rejected the practice of war.

1867-   The Indian Peace Commission negotiated final treaties with the
1868   Indians by signing the 370th pact on August 13, 1868, with the
           Nez Perces.

1867-   This was the era of mission to the Indians in Alaska. Many
1883   mainland churches established schools throughout this period.
           Included were Congregational, Episcopalian, Moravian, Pres-
           byterian, Roman Catholic and Swedish Evangelical churches.

1868   Indians were barred by the 14th Amendment, Section 2, from
           enjoying rights then accorded to the black man. The Indian was
           specifically denied the vote by the clause "excluding Indians not
           taxed," and had to wait almost sixty years for rights given to
           most other Americans.

           Under the Treaty of 1868, 24,000 square miles were set aside
           as the Navajo Reservation in Arizona, Colorado, New Mexico
           and Utah. An important provision of the treaty stipulated: "The
           United States agrees that for every 30 children...who can be
           induced or compelled to attend school, a house shall be pro-
           vided, and a teacher competent to teach the elementary branches
           of an English education shall be furnished...." Years of fail-
           ure and neglect followed and contributed to the result which dur-
           ing World War II saw the Selective Service System classify as
           illiterate 88 percent of Navajo males 18 to 35 years of age.
           This shameful omission forced white and Indian authorities to
           face the seriousness of their common problems and tremendous
           strides have since been taken to overcome the deficiency.

           The U.S. signed a treaty with the Dakotas, giving them the coun-
           try north of the North Platt River. This area was to have been
           their property forever, and under the treaty no whites were to
           be permitted to travel over their land or to settle there with-
           out permission. This treaty was soon broken. Gold was dis-
           covered, and trespassing prospectors in the Black Hills urged
           the government to resolve their troubles. The government of-
           fered the Indians $6,000,000 but the Indians wearily asked for
           $50 million as a figure being more nearly worth the trouble and
           indicative of the true land value.

1869   President U. S. Grant asked religious groups to propose names
           for Indian agency superintendents. (The practice was stopped
           a few years later.)

Congress passed the Act creating the Board of Indian Commissioners, which remained in operation until 1933.

President Grant's Quaker policy was instituted for the Indians.

Brig. General Ely Samuel Parker (Do-Ne-Ho-Geh-Weh), a chief from the Tonowanda-Seneca Tribe, was appointed on April 21 to become Commissioner of Indian Affairs by President Grant. He served until December, 1871.

The Bannocks (Shoshone-Northern Paiutes), who had given the white man no trouble, agreed to go to the Fort Hall Reservation in Idaho.

A sadder and decimated group of Navajos returned to Canyon de Chelly in Arizona after four years of banishment and virtual captivity in Fort Sumner, New Mexico.

The title to about fifty thousand acres of land upon which the Cherokees were living at Qualla, North Carolina, became involved in litigation brought about by the creditors of Colonel William Thomas. Thomas had been their benefactor and had purchased the land in his own name for them, but with Cherokee money. This occurred because state laws forbade the original Cherokee settlers (who had resisted attempts at resettlement from Georgia to Oklahoma by fleeing to the remote Carolina vastness) from owning their own ground. Eventually the federal government intervened to protect Cherokee interests. (Thomas had been a "front man" for the Indians in the land acquisitions from 1836 to 1861.)

1870   Congress provided the first specific appropriation for Indian education when it gave $100,000 for the operation of federal industrial schools.

About this time the Kiowa Indians seem to have had the cactus plant, peyote, introduced to them. Peyote produced a trance for the taker who usually had quite beautiful dreams with happy effects. Peyote was probably introduced by the Tonkawas and the Karankawas of Texas, who in turn probably learned about it in the nineteenth century from the Old Mexican tribes which used the druglike plant in ceremonials. A cult expansion followed, and today there exists a controversial Native American church group which evolved as an attempt to preserve their right to free use of peyote and resist any attempt to outlaw its use. While there are claims for cures for sicknesses, its principal use appears to be a form of escapism. While there are critics in large numbers, some advocates question whether the occasional use is worse than the curse of alcoholism introduced by corrupt white men. Some allege that Christian leaders use this controversial issue as a cover over an obvious threat to their approach and influence.

1870-1886   The Federal Indian policy of giving Indians food and clothing rations was started and implemented by military support, as gradually the remaining Indian tribes were gathered up and placed on reservations.

1871   U.S. Congress declared it would legislate the Indian tribes in the same manner as it did the white. Thus it abandoned the old policy of all Indian treaty-making by negotiation. Since that time, agreements with Indian groups have been made by Congressional Acts, Executive Orders and Executive Agreements.

The Act of March 3 makes provision for change of past procedures in "That hereafter no Indian Nation of Tribes within the territory of the United States shall be acknowledged or recognized as an independent nation, tribe or power with whom the United States may contract by treaty; provided further, that nothing herein shall be construed to invalidate or impair the obligations of any treaty heretofore lawfully made and ratified with any such Indian National or tribe." (16 Stats., 556)

1872   The members of the famous Powell Expedition became the first white men to explore the full length of the Grand Canyon, thanks to the assistance of the Poh-Ute Indians.

Indian Commissioner Francis A. Walker in Annual Report said: "There is no question of national dignity, be it remembered, involved in the treatment of the savages by a civilized power. With wild men as with wild beasts, the question whether in a given situation one shall fight, coax or run, is a question of merely what is easiest and safest...no one certainly will rejoice more heartily than the present commissioner when the Indians of this country cease to be in a position to dictate, in any form or degree to the government, when, in fact, the least hostile tribe becomes reduced to the condition of suppliants for charity."

Sisseton Sioux Indians (now of South Dakota) were persuaded
to sell 11 million acres of rich agricultural land in the Red River
Valley in Minnesota for a mere ten cents an acre.

1872-   The Modoc War was started with an attempt to arrest Chief
1873   Captain Jack for murdering a medicine man.

1873   Father Pierre Jean DeSmet, notable Indian missionary born in
           Belgium, died after a lifetime of service to the Sioux of the Da-
           kotas. He was the chief mediary between the United States gov-
           ernment and the Sioux at the time of the Red Cloud War. Many
           historians feel that no other white man had such a great influ-
           ence on the Indian peoples of that region.

           The federal government increased its interest in the establish-
           ment of government schools for Indians.

           Warm Springs Reservation for the Mimbreno Apaches was es-
           tablished near old Fort Cummings (now Cook's Springs, near
           Florida), New Mexico, causing the abandonment of that lonely
           frontier fort.

1874   In California, President Grant created Pyramid Lake Reserva-
           tion by Executive Order, setting aside the lake, one of America's
           largest natural bodies of water, as an Indian fishing place.

           Indians and white buffalo hunters fought a tragic battle in Texas
           during June, at the Adobe Wall Trading Post, over the Indian's
           desire to stop the white man's senseless destruction of buffalo
           in a wanton fashion. A small band of 20 white men and a single
           white woman were in the post when a force of approximately
           700 Comanche, Cheyenne and Kiowa-Apache, under Quanah
           Parker, attacked. The Indians were unable to attain their mis-
           sion because the whites were equipped with devastating buffalo
           guns which had long range and deadly accuracy. More than one
           hundred red men were killed in the affair, while only three
           white men are claimed to have lost their lives.

1875   Gold was discovered in the "Black Hills" of the Dakotas, which
           ultimately resulted in white entries and encroachments on Indian
           lands, and in red men attacks in a vain attempt to enforce their
           treaty with the federal government, whose agents sought only
           protection for the white miners and settlers.

1876   In Treaty No. 6, the Commissioner issued the following order: "A medicine chest will be kept in the house of the Indian Agent in case of sickness amongst you." Thus began health services for the Indians, meager as they were.

On June 25, the Battle of Grassy Grass or Little Big Horn, better known to white men as Custer's Massacre, took the lives of 266 men and "Yellow Hair" (Custer). This was a well-planned strategical and tactical battle by the military genius of the Sioux nation, Crazy Horse. According to the Sioux, Custer did not make any "last stand," but died early in the battle. The Indians deny the claim of white historians that Custer was "ringed by dead Sioux" by pointing out that their total dead in the battle was a mere twenty-two! Reviewing the affair from a tactical angle, one must conclude that the key to the Battle of the Little Big Horn was the Battle of Rosebud, which occurred ten days earlier. It was no accident that Crazy Horse was at Rosebud to meet General Crook, who was severely defeated and did not manage to move again for weeks. Although the Sioux knew from their spies of Custer's battle plans, they did not know he would split his force into three parts, with Benton and Reno being sent off into other directions to roam the hills. Thus the century-old debate over the wisdom of Custer in splitting his force is academic; for nothing could have prevented the battle, although the fray might have been prolonged if the troops had not been dismounted. Coincidental, too, was the fact that Custer turned his main body of men into the place where the Indians were best prepared for them and surrounded them without further movement.

Chief Joseph White Bull, a Miniconfou sub-chief of the Teton Sioux, drew an annotated account of his personal exploit in which he claimed to have killed Custer, which the historian Stanley Vestal accepts.

U.S. Congressman James Garrison claimed that the Secretary of the Interior had advised him that he would "rejoice as far as the Indian matter was concerned when the last buffalo was killed." He did not have to wait long as the wanton killings of the hunters decimated the herds. The Union Pacific Railroad cut the herds into northern and southern groups. In a two-month period, 260,000 buffalo were killed in one section, and there were so many hides on the market that the price fell to a mere one dollar per skin. By 1878 the southern herd was

virtually wiped out, with the last remnants fleeing to the Staked
Plains of Texas, where the last four were killed in 1889. The
northern group's demise was roughly parallel. In the period
1876 to 1882 the damage was done in a most inhumane fashion.
By 1883 there remained only a single small herd near Cannon
Ball River in North Dakota. That autumn, Sitting Bull headed
his warriors in the last winter hunt, in which approximately one
thousand were killed in a day. The next autumn there were no
animals left! This was one of the greatest blows to the red man,
for the buffalo had provided him with food, shelter and clothing. Not a single part of the animal was wasted by the Indian --
hair was used for reins, horns made drinking cups, etc.

1876-   The Sioux were fighting to keep out prospectors who were en-
1877   croaching on their lands and driving off cattle and other ani-
          mals, thus adding further agonies to people who were already
          living on short food rations doled out by white administrators.
          Led by such reknowned chiefs as Sitting Bull, Gall and Crazy
          Horse, the Indians were effective for a time, especially at the
          Battle of the Little Big Horn with Custer.

1877   The Nez Perce broke out of the reservation, led by Young Chief
          Joseph. When they were finally captured again, their punish-
          ment was to be sent to Oklahoma and to be banned from their
          old reservation for a time.

          The United States, by executive order, recognized the Pueblo
          grant of the Zuni holdings on March 16. On May 1, 1883, this
          order was amended by President Chester A. Arthur, and was
          repeated on March 3, 1885, defining and extending the Zuni res-
          ervation boundaries "to except lands already settled upon and
          occupied in good faith by white settlers." The reservation now
          comprises about 440,000 acres, mostly in McKinley County in
          New Mexico, with a small portion in the south lying in Valencia
          County.

1878   Congress approved the first appropriations for Indian police.

          Ending an era and spelling the doom of a proud people's culture
          and nomadic way of life, the Consolidated Barbed Wire Com-
          pany of Lawrence, Kansas shipped their product to five states
          in order to "fence the prairies."

Hampton Normal, an Agricultural Institute in Virginia, began to accept Indian students through the efforts of General R.H. Pratt (later the founder of Carlisle Indian School). In the following twelve years a total of 460 were trained there. Fortunately, for later researchers, that institution kept records of their students as they went back to their reservations. The records showed that the adjustments made were graded as being: "Excellent, 98; Good, 219; Fair, 91; Poor, 35; Bad, 17."

Of a reported 1,735 Chippewa Indians who had been allotted land around 1871, five-sixths of them had either sold their land or had been defrauded of it by unscrupulous whites.

The Bannocks, angered by the loss of their hunting grounds and the effect of the white man's depredations upon the buffalo, started the uprising known as the Bannock War. The military campaign to subdue and return them was led by General O.O. Howard, After their defeat, they lived on their reservation harmoniously without any major incidents marring the tranquility.

1879   The Utes went on the warpath, but it was short lived, and Chief Oury had to sign away all their Colorado land as a price for peace and punishment for the caprice. They had killed the White River agent, who had been forcing them into farming.

Carlisle Indian School was established at Fort Carlisle, Pennsylvania, by Captain Richard H. Pratt, thereby starting a more effective educational and vocational training system. By 1900 there were twelve hundred pupils enrolled from seventy-nine tribes. Pratt's ideas are to be noted from some of his thoughts and words: "To civilize the Indian, put him in the midst of civilization. To keep him civilized, keep him there."

1881   The great Sioux chieftan, Spotted Tail, died in South Dakota.

The number of Indian schools was reported to be 106.

Nana, aged lieutenant of the feared Victoriano, staged a phenomenal raid in New Mexico which caused the reactivation of abandoned Fort Cummings. In July and August Nana plundered the southern and western parts of New Mexico, sweeping down on remote ranches, killing civilians, carrying off livestock and women and eluding his pursuers. After he had won eight running battles with soldiers, Nana escaped practically untouched into Mexico.

Congress considered a bill to compel Indian tribes to divide their tribal land holdings among their individual members. This became the forerunner of attempts still being made to enable the dominant white men to gain control of land which they could not get by other means.

1881-   Despite safeguards in the Bill of Rights of the Constitution, Pres-
1885   ident Chester A. Arthur authorized the Secretary of the Interior
         to give official approval to rules forbidding "rites, customs...
         contrary to civilization." In the same action dances, religious
         rites and traditional rituals were likewise forbidden.

1882   The Indian Rights Association was founded.

         Congress passed laws to convert army forts into Indian schools.

         Arizona Territory Apaches made enough rumblings so that the
         old Indian fighter, General Crook -- known variously as "Three
         Stars" to the Plains Indians, and "Gray Fox" to the Apaches --
         was sent back to the territory to investigate the causes for Indian
         unrest. His findings were mitigated by the efforts of a ring of
         corrupt white contractors in Tucson, who did not want the Indians
         to become self-supporting. There were rumors that the Apaches
         would be driven out of their reservation at San Carlos. Other
         rumors that coal and silver had been found, coupled with the
         possibility of the advent of the railroad, encouraged greedy
         white men, who again attempted to dispossess the Apache.

1883   Courts for Indian offenses on Indian reservations were estab-
         lished. The new courts were given the authority to try infrac-
         tions of rules laid down by the Interior Department for the
         running of the reservations.

         The Bureau of Indian Affairs awarded a contract to Sergeant
         and Lewis of Topeka, Kansas, to build the first three buildings
         for the projected Indian Industrial Training School in Lawrence,
         Kansas.

1884   Haskell Institute in Lawrence, Kansas, and Chilocco Indian
         School in Oklahoma opened to provide vocational training, thus

marking the start of programs of education and land resource development for Indians by the government. Haskell's dedication took place on September 17, with Dr. James Marvin, ex-Chancellor of the University of Kansas, taking office as Superintendent. That day twenty-two Pawnee children were enrolled: and a few days later on September 20, eight Arapaho and Cheyenne chiefs brought an additional eighty youngsters to enroll.

Congress appropriated funds for education in Alaska, directing that they be distributed among the existing mission schools. The following year, Dr. Sheldon Jackson was appointed as general agent for education in Alaska.

By the Act of May 17, native Indian rights were clearly recognized when Congress provided for a civil government in the Territory of Alaska. Definitions were left to a future Congress to spell out.

The U.S. Congress acknowledged the rights of the native Eskimos to Alaskan territorial lands. Since that time, the Eskimos have never sold their rights or lost them through war, and have never given them away by treaty. Numerous legislative proposals are stalled in Congress for an orderly development of millions of acres of land claims. One newspaper described the 53,000 Eskimos, Indians and Aleutian Islanders as "probably the nation's poorest citizens." Many persons argue, with good authority, that Alaska has been the known habitat of the Eskimos since their advent on this continent. At a recent $900 million sale of North Slope oil leases in Anchorage, picketers marched outside the auditorium denouncing the transactions as "economic genocide."

1885   It was Washington Matthews (Navajo) who first recorded some of the sand paintings and songs of the Navajos. These were published in an ethnological report of that time.

The last great herd of buffalo was exterminated.

President U.S. Grant signed into law the bill which resulted in the withdrawal of federal troops guarding the borders of the Indian Territory (now Oklahoma). It was not long before "boomers" and "sooners" flocked into the region, resulting in an early white population of 60,000.

Publication of Helen Hunt Jackson's book, <u>A Century of Dishonor</u>, aroused the nation to improve the conditions of the Indians.

1886   A Congressional Act provided that particular crimes committed by Indians on reservations were to be heard in the U.S. District Courts.

The Apaches in Arizona under Geronimo and Nachez, another great leader, surrendered and agreed to peace. Later the Apaches were resettled in the Indian Territory in Oklahoma. (Negotiations dragged on for several months, during which time General Crook resigned in disgust. The Indians finally were ready to sign, only to be given "fire water" by renegade whites, after which they broke out of the reservation.)

1887   Congress passed an Act giving the President the power to divide any Indian Reservation into separate allotments, over which a twenty-five year trusteeship was to be applied. Remaining surplus and unallocated lands were to be disposed of. This unfair action squeezed the Indians from 155,000,000 acres into a mere 47,000,000 acres. (This was later modified by the Indian Reorganization Act of 1934.)

The Dawes, or General Allotment Act, went into effect on February 7. It gave severalty land to individual Indians in an effort to discourage them from living in tribes. It authorized the President to subdivide tribally owned lands into individual plats <u>without</u> the consent of the Indian tribe affected. The intent of the Allotment Act was to assimilate the Indian by giving him individual ownership of land, as opposed to traditional collective land use and possession practiced at that time by most Indian tribes and pueblos. Vast areas of Indian land were soon lost forever. It is to be noted that even then there were many who opposed the Act on grounds that it might be forced on large groups of Indians who were not ready for such a drastic change.

1888   Congress directed the Board of Education in Alaska to set up a course of study for all government schools.

1889   During the summer General George Crook negotiated the last Indian Treaty. By the terms of this treaty, which affected three-fourths of the adults of the bands involved, the Indians relinquished all lands between the White and the Cheyenne Rivers, as well as what are now the four counties of Perkins, Harding,

and parts of Meade and Butte, in South Dakota. The treaty became effective February 10, 1890.

At noon, April 22, a boundary line marked by flags and stretching as far as the eye could see separated a drawn-up conglom-
eration of wheeled vehicles, buckboards, surreys, connestogas,
coaches and bicycles from the vast Indian Territory of Oklahoma, closed by law to white settlers...until that moment.
With tremendous din, the white men, with their horses, dogs and
cows, raised a vast cloud of dust as they raced to stake their
claims on choice acreages. 50,000 persons went past the line
on that day. By nightfall there were tent cities, banks and stores
doing business. Each year the Oklahomans revive the event with
huge parades, rodeos, and general pandemonium in celebration
of "the run of 1889."

1890   Unarmed Sioux men, women and children were massacred by
            federal troops at the infamous Battle of Wounded Knee.

            Old Comanche War Chief Quanah Parker, having surrendered in
            1875 to become a virtual collaborator in white government pol-
            icies, had been appointed a judge, but was relieved of his duties
            for having broken the white man's law by possessing too many
            wives, which violated the codes of the Courts of Indian Offenses.

            Congress enacted laws to cover the costs of tuition of Indians
            attending public schools.

1890-   The Ghost Dance Movement arose, flourished, influenced many
1891   tribes and then withered away. Wovoka, or Jake Wilson, a Paiute
            medicine man who claimed to have had a meeting with the Great
            Spirit while he was ill and unconscious, preached to his people
            that the plains would again support vast herds of buffalo, and
            the white man and his ways would go away. Force and violence
            were not favored, but rather dancing and songs to speed the
            coming of that welcome day. There was much agitation and
            action; but even the unfortunate death of Sitting Bull, when the
            whites tried to take him prisoner, did not start a great and
            general uprising as anticipated by alarmist whites.

1891   The ending of the Indian Wars witnessed a vast decline in the
            number of scouts in the Army. In 1891 the figure had fallen to
            150, with the reduction continuing until 1915 when there were

only 24 on active duty. One of the many duties of the scouts during the Indian campaigns was to supply the Army posts with fresh meat.

1893   The need for water for livestock on the Navajo reservation became so acute that Congress appropriated the first funds for Indian water development.

A Senatorial commission laid the ground for the introduction of "severalty" among the Five Civilized Tribes, after cautiously choosing its witnesses.

The Indian Appropriations Act contained the first provision to eliminate the Indian Agent, transferring control to the Superintendent of Schools located on the reservation. By this Act, the Superintendent of the Indian School at Cherokee, North Carolina, was required in addition to his regular duties to perform those formerly done by the Agent for the Cherokee Agency. By this means, the number of Indian Agencies was gradually diminished, until in 1907 only a single one, located in Wintah, Utah, remained.

1894   Haskell Institute grew to the point where nine grades were required for their pupils.

1895   Anton Dvorak wrote The New World Symphony, utilizing the music of the Omaha (Nebraska) Indians as a theme. Included were such selections as Land of the Sky Blue Waters and At Dawning.

1896   Haskell Institute attempted to meet the needs of the Indians by offering a kindergarten course.

1899   Meeting pressures from various groups, the Bureau of Indian Affairs authorized religious groups to conduct religious services and training at Indian schools for periods not to exceed three hours a week.

Local communities in Alaska were authorized by the Bureau of Indian Affairs and Congress to set up school boards.

$2,500,000 annually was being expended for education at 148 boarding schools and 225 day schools for 20,000 Indian students.

A monument was erected by the Colonial Dames of America in Savannah, Georgia, to the memory of Tomochichi, noted Creek chief who had helped in founding the Georgia Colony.

1900   On November 4, 300 Oneida Indians went to the polls and voted in the New York State elections.

        The Bureau of Census reported that Indian illiteracy was 56 percent. With the rise in educational opportunities, that figure dropped to 25 percent in 1930 and to an estimated 12 percent in 1959. (Comparable data from the 1960 census are not available.)

1902   The first local school board was established at Nome, Alaska. Thus a step toward making Indian-Aleut-Eskimo education more relevant was taken.

1902-   A new approach was enacted with Federal Indian reclamation,
1910   forestry and conservation programs.

1903   Many Indian agencies were eliminated and their work load shifted to the reservation schools as the start of a temporary trend along those lines.

        "Chief" Charles Bender (Chippewa) started his major league baseball career with the Philadelphia Athletics of the American League. Considered one of the great pitchers of all times, he won 212 games while losing only 28.

1904   The government started to allot lands to the Sioux in South Dakota.

1905   A canal was built to divert a portion of the water from the Truckee River to the Newlands Reservation for the benefit of white settlers in Nevada.

1906   The Burke Act withheld citizenship from the Indians until the Government Trust period expired.

        The Cutbank Canal, serving the Blackfeet Reservation of the Blackfeet and Peigan Indians of Montana, was completed by the Indian Service, using mostly Indian labor and teams of horses in the irrigation project encompassing 14,000 acres of land.

        The Federal Government seized 50,000 acres of wilderness land high in the Sangre de Cristo mountains of New Mexico and included it in their creation of the Carson National Park. This land was considered sacred by the Taos Indian Pueblo, which regarded the area much as a white man reveres his church. Blue Lake is a principal shrine of the Taos religion.

1907   With the growth of Oklahoma to the stature of statehood, many
            Indians, including Benjamin Harrison, a Choctaw, helped draw
            up the new state's constitution.

            Tribesmen gathered at Sheridan, Wyoming, and buried their
            bitter feelings by staging a goodwill show. From this has come
            the annual All American Indian Days celebrations, in which the
            Indian tribes of the area and the non-Indian community at Sheri-
            dan cooperate.

            Charles Curtis of Kansas was honored by election to the U.S.
            Senate, thereby becoming the first Indian to attain such high
            rank and prominence. He served from January 23 to March 13,
            1913, and from March 4, 1915 to March 3, 1929, when he re-
            signed to step up to the Vice-Presidency.

1908   The title "Indian Agent" was abandoned and gradually the term
            "Superintendent" came into use. This position is usually filled
            through promotion of Bureau of Indian Affairs career workers.

            Louis Tewanima, a Hopi Indian from Arizona, competed in the
            Olympic Games held in London and finished ninth in the 26-mile
            distance affair. In the next Olympics, he finished second to the
            famed "Flying Finn," Kannes Kilehmainen. He was a triple
            medal winner in both the 1908 and 1912 Olympics, in which he
            competed in both the 5 and 10,000 meter, as well as the mara-
            thon races. He was the first athlete to be elected to the Ari-
            zona Sports Hall of Fame.

1909   Provision was made for a Medical Supervisor within the Indian
            Bureau.

1910   The Omnibus Act made provisions for the determination of heirs
            of allottees, holdings of trust patents on land, partition of es-
            tates, issuance of certificates of competency to individual In-
            dians, making of Indian wills, prohibition of conveyance of trust
            land, protection of Indian timber and various allotment pro-
            cedures.

            The Medical Division was originated and located within the
            Indian Service.

            Bureau of Indian Affairs regulations forbade the Sun Dance of
            the Plains Indians because of the extreme self-torture perpe-
            trated by dance participants. There were flagrant violations

of the U.S. Constitution, in which the Bureau lent itself to the suppression of Indian religions, whether or not the tribe practiced torture. Later, in 1934, religious freedom was finally recognized.

1911   The last recorded uprising of Indians occurred when the heretofore peaceful Shoshones, who had never raised a finger against the white man, revolted in Humbolt County, Nevada. A few Indian renegades murdered some stockmen. The sheriff's posse, which hunted down the band, butchered everyone except an Indian woman and two small children. (No one seems to have recorded why they were spared.)

Indian Commissioner Robert G. Valentine reported, "Indian Affairs are, even under the best possible administration, peculiarly a field for the grafter and other wrongdoers. The land and the monies of the Indian offer a bait which the most saited will not refuse."

1912   "The Osage (Okla.) Tribe held the first public auction sale for oil leases on Osage Reservation tracts November 11. Early sales were held under this elm tree...The first sale in which a 160 acre tract brought a bonus of $1,000,000, or more was March 2, 1922. One tract brought $1,335,000 and another tract brought $1,160,000. On March 18, 1924 the opening bid on a 160 acre tract was $1,000,000. However, the largest bonus ever paid for a tract was $1,990,000 on March 19, 1924. A total of 18, 160 acre tracts for a bonus of over $1,000,000 have been leased, thus this tree under which these high bids were made became known as the 'Million Dollar Elm'."(Plaque at Osage Agency in Pawhuska.)

Jim Thorpe, of the Sauk and Fox Tribe, represented the United States in the Olympic games in which he won the decathalon. The Carlisle Institute graduate has often been referred to as the world's greatest athlete.

The first Navajo dictionary ever published was compiled by the Franciscan Fathers of Arizona. The book subsequently became so rare that the Navajos themselves do not have a copy. (One is to be found in the private museum of Wright's Trading Post, owned by Mr. and Mrs. S.A. Chernoff, 616 Gold Street, S. W., Albuquerque, New Mexico, 87107.)

1913   The federal government issued the famous "Buffalo Head" Indian nickel designed by James Earl Fraser. This was an idealized composite portrait of thirteen Indian chiefs, including John Big

Tree of the Iroquois, Iron Tail of the Sioux and Two Moons of the Cheyenne. In May of 1966, Chief Big Tree was still alive on the Onondaga Reservation near Syracuse, New York.

1915   Congress passed the first appropriation act authorizing the Indian Bureau to buy land for landless Indians in the State of California.

1916   On May 5 the U.S. Army Indian Scouts fought their last fight at the Ojos Azules Ranch, approximately 300 miles below the Mexican borderline. An Apache Scout detachment was part of the 11th Cavalry, which fought an indecisive battle against elements of Pancho Villa's forces. Although the main body of the Villa force escaped, they left behind forty-four killed and many more wounded. No American soldiers were even scratched in the fray.

May 13 was set aside as Indian Day, and was sponsored by the Society of American Indians. The purpose was to recognize and honor the American Indian, and to improve his conditions. It is not a national holiday.

1917   Revising an Indian demographic trend of over fifty years, it was revealed that for the first time in that period births exceeded deaths.

Congress abolished the practice of payment of subsidies to religious groups for the education of Indians.

In a "Declaration of Policy" statement issued by Interior Department Secretary Franklin Land and Bureau of Indian Affairs Commissioner Cato Sells, it was stated, "The time has come for discontinuing guardianship over all competent Indians and giving even closer attention to the incompetents that they more speedily achieve competency." Commissioner Sells applauded the new policy as an indication that "the competent Indian will no longer be treated as half ward and half citizen."

1917-   Despite their not being subject to the draft law, more than 8,000
1918   Indians served in World War I, of whom some 6,000 were volunteers. This was later to be a serious factor in the decision of the Congress to pass the Indian Citizenship Act of 1924.

1918   The First American (Indian) Church was incorporated on October 10 at El Reno, Oklahoma, by Mack Hoag of the Cheyenne tribe, and other members from the Otto, Ponca, Commanche, Kiowa and Apache tribes.

1919   A Congressional inquiry into the progress of Navajo education revealed that of an estimated 9,613 children of school age, only 2,089 were acutally in school. When the facts became known the following year, the Secretary of the Interior was ordered to "make and enforce such rules and regulations as may be necessary to secure the enrollment and regular attendance of eligible Indian children." Later, investigators found that for years afterward, not more than one-half of the school-age children were enrolled. The celebrated Meriam Report of 1928 also points to this condition.

1921   John Levi, star athlete and student at Haskell Institute, became one of the first Indians to be named to the All American football team that year.

1922   A dam was built to divert the entire flow of the Truckee River from the Indian benefits, and the excess water was callously flushed away into a swamp.

In November, for the first time since they drove the Spaniards out of New Mexico in 1680, all of the Rio Grande Pueblos met and joined forces to resist the proposed Bursum bill, which would have legislated rights for white squatters on Pueblo lands. The unexpected outcome was that public opinion supported the Indians and caused the creation of the Pueblo Land Board to safeguard Indian rights, and to so establish an equitable method for ascertaining land ownership in areas of dispute.

The annual Gallup Inter-Tribal Indian Ceremonials, which attract tribesmen from all parts of the nation and even some from Old Mexico and Canada, opened for the first time in New Mexico on the second Thursday in August and continued for four days. Thus began the event which brings tribes together for fun, feasting, dancing and contests of all sorts, restricted to Indians, but closely watched by "palefaces" from all over the world. They come to listen to the representation of many cultural backgrounds, to view the fine examples of Navajo rugs, Hopi kachina dolls, pottery, silver and turquoise jewelry and other handmade items, and to generally mingle amidst a carefree world of yesterday and today. Into Gallup, "Indian Capital of the World," now pour thousands of on-lookers each year as a result of this event, and it brings needed cash income to the Indians. In 1970, the ceremonials were housed on a modern set of grounds which replaced the old ones torn down to make way for interstate traffic.

1923   Victor Manuel (Pima), a printer, became one of the organizers of Arizona Printers, Inc., a thriving publishing house in that area.

A committee of one hundred was appointed by the Secretary of the Interior after public furor arose regarding a plan to take away land from the Rio Grande Pueblos. The committee devoted much time to health and similar problems of the red man.

The Territory of Alaska tried unsuccessfully to enact a law prohibiting enrollment of Indian children in their public schools.

A survey of the United States Commissioner of Education revealed that "only 14 percent of the Indian children in Oklahoma were enrolled in the public school system of that state."

1924   By an Act of Congress of June 2, American citizenship was conferred on Indians (43 Stat L 253) which stated that "all non-citizen Indians born within the territorial limits of the U.S. be, and are hereby declared to be, citizens of the United States."

The Indian Health Division was created within the Indian Bureau.

1926   Phillip Osif, who had attended Haskell Institute, and was National Six Mile Track champion, became a member of the U.S. Olympic Games Team.

The Government boarding school for Indians at White Mountain, Alaska, was renamed "Industrial School." This was the inception of a policy and program of industrial training for boarding school students.

A Pima Indian died whose land allotment from the tribe amounted to twenty acres in the Gila River Reservation of Arizona. His estate was divided among seventy-three persons. The largest interest amounted to one acre, while several persons received pieces of ground eleven feet square!

1928   Charles Curtis of Kansas, Kaw tribe, a U.S. Senator for 25 years, was elected Vice President of the United States to serve in the Hoover administration.

The Lewis Meriam Associates Report, issued during the administration of President Herbert Hoover, provided the basis for three different policies of administering Indian affairs by Hoover's successors.

The first motion picture was taken of the Navajo Mountain Chant by Laura Adams Armer (Hosteen Tsosi).

1930   The U.S. Senate Investigating Committee exposed conditions which revealed virtual systematic kidnapping of Indian children from their Navajo parents on the reservation by the B.I.A. school officials.

1930-   Winter saw the Sioux and other Indian tribes saved from starva-
1931   tion by contributions of private citizens and emergency actions of the Red Cross.

1930's   In the late part of this decade, the Navajo system of writing, known as the Harrington-LaFarge alphabet, was devised and introduced to the Southwest tribe who live primarily in a four-state region of Arizona, Colorado, New Mexico and Utah.

         The latter part of this decade saw Navajo grazing allotments reduced by the government from one million sheep units to 750,000 because of the condition of the overgrazed and eroded lands. This act impoverished some Navajo families.

1931   Administration of education among the natives of Alaska was transferred to the Office of Indian Affairs, headquartered in Juneau. Gradually the office became known as the Alaska Indian Service.

1932   The Alaska Indian Service opened the Wrangle Institute Boarding School.

1933   John Collier was appointed Commissioner of Indian Affairs by President Franklin Roosevelt. Collier was, to many, "a new era of hope with his Indian Reorganization Act," which gave local government to tribes which requested it. To others, his was a regime of the return of the Indian "to the blanket."

1934   The Johnson-O'Malley Act passed by Congress caused many facets of Indian administration to be assigned to numerous federal agencies. The act authorized the Secretary of the Interior to enter into contracts with states for the education of Indians, and to permit the use of federal school buildings and equipment by local school authorities. As a result, there are some states with enormous Indian populations which have no federal schools within their boundaries.

The Indian Reorganization Act of 1934, the work of Commissioner John Collier, aimed to provide the Indians the greatest measure of control of their tribal lands and affairs up to that time.

The Wheeler-Howard Indian Reorganization Act reversed the trend to split up Indian land holdings. It provided for tribal ownership and self-government.

1935   On January 24, the Santa Clara Pueblo in New Mexico celebrated the adoption of a constitution for the pueblo and the election of pueblo officers under the constitution. Adoption came after more than fifty years of pueblo unrest. Weeks of polite argument, conciliations, and concessions by every faction preceded adoption. There were times in the long course of those meetings when white observers felt it was hopeless. Little by little, though, with a tenacity and self-control which many white villages would be unable to emulate, the Santa Clarans worked out their difficulties until at last the matter was concluded and practically everyone in the pueblo supported the new constitution.

1936   With enactment of the Oklahoma Welfare Act, that state provided for the organization of Indian tribes within their state.

The Indian Arts and Crafts Board, enacted by Congress in 1935, was established. In this action Congress gave official recognition to Indian culture, and instructed the Board to encourage Indians to turn certain aspects of the culture to commercial advantage. A fine, imprisonment, or both, may be imposed on businessmen who misrepresent imitation Indian art and craft products as being authentic Indian crafts.

Appearing with the U.S. Olympic Games Team in Berlin was Wilson "Buster" Charles, star Haskell athlete.

1937   The Papago Tribal Council was organized and a constitution and set of by-laws adopted.

1938   The Pimas were organized with a constitution and by-laws recognized by the Bureau of Indian Affairs.

The Government had acquired 657,526 acres of land as a result of the 1937 Bankhead-Jones Act, commonly known as Title III, Land Utilization Lands. Most of the lands were located in northern New Mexico, but the federal authorities set aside some of the Ojo del Espiritu Santo Grant acreage which they had acquired in 1934 for the Jemez Pueblo, and other land acquired for the Zia Pueblo. The Indians had considered prior claims as spurious and were shocked to hear that they had been historically using land actually "clouded" as to rightful possession. The land was transferred in trust for the Pueblos, who have been buying back parts of the grant ever since.

1939 Roman Catholic beatification of an American Indian occurred On May 9, when the Cardinals in Rome recommended the beatification of Kateritekawitha, "the lily of the Mohawks," who was born in 1656 at Ossernenon, New York. The decision was approved by Pope Pius XII on May 19.

The Sioux Museum and Crafts Center was created by the joint sponsorship of the federal government and Rapid City, South Dakota. The museum is administered by the Indian Arts and Crafts Board, an agency of the U.S. Department of Interior.

The Havasupai in Arizona organized a Tribal Council.

1940 In October, the Haskell Institute unit of the Kansas National Guard was mobilized and entered into one year's active federal service.

In October, for the first time in United States history, American Indians registered for "the draft."

1941 The U.S. Supreme Court restored 509,000 acres of land to the Hualapai Indians of Arizona, in the case of The United States as Guardian of Hualapai v. Santa Fe Pacific Railroad Company 314 U.S. 339.

Dillon S. Meyer reversed the Collier policy during the Truman administration. The Indian Bureau returned to the policy of paternalism and domination.

1941- During the events of World War II, more than 25,000 Indian men
1945 and women were enrolled in the military services. They served on all fronts in the conflict during which they were honored by receiving 71 Air Medals, 51 Silver Stars, 47 Bronze Stars, 34 Distinguished Flying Crosses and two Congressional Medals of Honor. Their most famed exploit was that of the Navajo Marines, who used their language as a battlefield code which the enemy failed to break. In all, about 70,000 Indian men and women left reservations for the first time, to enter military

service or the defense industries. This brought about new vocational skills and an increased degree of cultural sophistication and awareness in dealing with non-Indians.

1942   A January 9 press release revealed that 40 percent more Indians enlisted than had been drafted to that date.

1944   The Truckee River Decree was enacted to protect the Indians by returning first and second rights on the water flow, but there was no tangible ruling to accompany the decree. (When General John C. Fremont visited Lake Pyramid it was over 220 square miles in area, but by 1944 it had shrunk to less than fifty.)

A History of Proposed Settlement Claims of California Indians was written by Robert W. King, Attorney General for the State of California.

William Stigler (Choctaw) was elected to the U.S. Congress from Oklahoma, and served in the 78th-82nd Congresses. Born in Tallequah, Oklahoma, July 7, 1891, he was graduated from Northeastern State College in 1912. He served as City Attorney in Stigler from 1920 to 1924, became State Senator in 1924 and served until 1932. He served as a 2nd Lt. in the AEF, and died on August 21, 1952.

1945   The name of the Alaska Indian Service was officially changed to "Alaska Native Service," presumably to more accurately describe its functions and clients.

1946   The Indian Claims Commission was created by an Act of Congress to settle land claims. (It was thought that only five to ten years would be required to adequately remove this long standing vexation.) Before this commission was created, claims of tribes, bands and other groups against the United States could only be brought before the court if specifically authorized in each instance by Congress. To date almost 600 claims have been filed with the Indian Claims Commission.

Only about 6,000 or 25 percent of the Navajo children between the ages of 6 and 18 years were in school. An estimated 18,000, or 75 percent were not.

1947   Army Indian Scouts were discontinued as a distinct element of the military forces of the United States. The last members had been serving at Fort Huachucha, Arizona. Their last duties had included patrolling the boundaries of the post to keep out trespassers and serving as guides for surveying parties from the Interior Department. Numerous Indian heroes of the wars received the Congressional Medal of Honor for their bravery. Achesay, Blanquet, Chiquito, Elaatoosu, Jim, Kelsay, Kosaha, Machol, Nannasaddie and Nantajie, for instance, were some who were decorated during the Indian Wars for "gallant conduct during the campaigns and engagements with the Apaches."

1948   Five Indians, survivors of the battle of the Little Big Horn, were among participants in the June 3 dedication of the Crazy Horse Monument in South Dakota, which was started by sculpter Korczak Ziolkowski, and will be completed with the help of contributions from interested private individuals and groups. The monument, which will take up an entire mountain top and be visible from all directions, is part of a plan which includes a research center, a medical school for Indians, etc.

Disenfranchising interpretations of the Arizona and New Mexico State constitutions were declared "unconstitutional" by court decrees, and the Indians were given the right to vote as they did in other states.

An Act was passed by Congress permitting the Secretary of the Interior to grant rights-of-way over Indian lands with the consent of the tribal authorities.

1949   The Hoover Commission on Reorganization of Government recommended the Termination Policy for Indians.

The State of Arizona, even as late as this year, refused to include Indians in any of its relief programs, nor would they permit Indian children to be assisted by crippled children's programs, a policy which persisted for years thereafter.

Emory S. Sekaquattawa, a Navajo, was admitted to the United States Military Academy from the State of Arizona on July 1, thereby becoming the second Indian to qualify for that demanding institution.

1950   In the dawning years of America's entry into the "space age," a Bureau of Indian Affairs survey estimated that America's first citizens, the Indians, still had 19,300 children for whom there was no school training of any kind.

The superintendent of the Blackfoot Reservation in Montana tried to continue outmoded paternalistic habits of white overseers by forbidding the Indians from playing gambling games after six P.M. The "old ones" were playing the Indian equivalents of such inconsequential games as bridge, gin rummy and canasta, and staying up late! The Indians had to have help from their lawyer in order to get the ridiculous regulation revoked.

The Johnson-O'Malley Act provided for the transfer of schools in Alaska to the administrative control of the territorial government.

An additional step was taken to increase the educational program provided for Indian children when the "Bordertown" program was originated, in which dormitory students attended local public high schools.

Dillon S. Meyer became Commissioner of Indian Affairs and supported the concepts of the new "termination" policy of the B.I.A.

1951   The Paiutes (a language brother of the Hopi tribe) organized a Tribal Council as a way to deal more effectively with the changing times and ways of life in a white-dominated society.

Annie Dodge Wauneka broke with tribal tradition when she was elected the first Navajo woman to the Tribal Council which was composed of only seventy-four members.

1952   The "Revolving Loan Fund" still had funds; however, the B.I.A. simply stopped making loans from it.

The Bureau of Indian Affairs inaugurated a program of employment assistance which gave opportunities to Indians who wished to relocate in urban communities or to find work on or near a reservation, and to obtain adult vocational training in school or on-the-job training programs. Included in this program were provisions for financial help and assistance on how a family could adjust to a new environment. Over 62,000 Indians have received aid from this program.

1953   Indians of the State of Maine who were not under federal jurisdiction were given the right to vote.

Miss Arlene Wesley James, a Yakima from Washington, became Miss Indian America I as the result of winning the important featured event at the annual All American Indian Days celebration at Sheridan, Wyoming. Like the Atlantic City, N.J.

competition for the title of Miss America, contestants are judged on the basis of poise, Indian characteristics, scholastic ability and dedication to the advancement of the Indian people. They represent many tribes from throughout the United States and Canada. Winners travel widely to represent the American Indian people as goodwill ambassadors at many national and international events.

The odious P.L. 280 was passed by Congress, empowering any state by an act of its own legislature to take over civil and criminal jurisdiction on Indian reservations, without consent of the tribes! The law specified that Indian lands in a few states (including those of the Omahas in Nebraska) were automatically removed from federal and placed under state jurisdiction. This put an end to Indian authority to police themselves.

An Act of Congress removed the old prohibition of off-reservation sales of liquor to Indians.

The Joint Congressional Resolution calling for federal termination of Indian lands was heard. It provided: "It is the policy of Congress, as rapidly as possible, to make the Indians within the territorial limits of the United States subject to the same laws and entitled to the same privileges and responsibilities as are applicable to other citizens of the United States, and to end their status as wards of the United States, and to grant them all the rights and prerogatives pertaining to citizenship...."

1954   A modern-day Abe Lincoln was personified in the person of Woody Yellowhorse, a Navajo, who in September walked 40 miles to enroll in Haskell Institute. He had to walk the long distance when he missed the last bus from his home in Arizona to the bus station in Tuba City.

The Menominees of Wisconsin, on June 17, were involved in the first of several acts which called for the end of federal trust of Indian lands. The Menominee tribe had a big investment in forest lands and a tribal sawmill. Final termination was delayed until April 30, 1961.

The Bureau of Indian Affairs tried in vain to disestablish its responsibility for the Choctaw Indians of Mississippi, when it entered into a contract with the state to take over its agricultural extension service, and sought to ignore the fact that federal provisions required against racial discrimination had not been included in the contract. Fortunately, the waiver was discovered at the White House, and there was no approval.

1955   In July, Congress under P.L. 568 ordered the Public Health Service to raise Indian health to a level comparable to that of the nation as a whole.

The Division of Indian Health transferred from the Department of the Interior to the new Health, Education and Welfare Department, so that all assets of HEW could be brought to bear upon and solve the health problems of the Indians.

1956   The Alaska Native Service was transferred to the jurisdiction and control of the Bureau of Indian Affairs.

The Bureau of Indian Affairs started an adult education program aimed at, among other things, increasing adult functional literacy. In fiscal year 1967, more than 12,000 adult Indians were in formal classes for basic education or high school equivalency.

1957   "We Shake Hands", a demonstration project supervised by the Association of American Indian Affairs, was established by certain Omaha, Sioux and Winnibago leaders to overcome reactionary federal Indian policies which discouraged Indians. It provided a framework for observable long-range programs of community action in Great Plains reservations. Later it was expanded to include cooperative local and non-Indian volunteers so essential to success. This project is still extant.

Congress ordered the Public Health Service to provide additional financial assistance for the construction of community hospitals serving both Indians and non-Indians, if, in the opinion of the Surgeon General, such construction would constitute a more effective way of providing hospital facilities for Indians. (PL 85-151)

1958   Leo Johnson of Fairfax, Oklahoma, matriculated at the Air Force Academy on June 12, thereby becoming the first Indian to enter that select body of young Americans. He was graduated and commissioned in the Air Force on June 6, 1962. He is presently a captain and is an RC 135-M pilot. Captain Johnson has received seven Air Medals and the Air Force Commendation Medal.

Secretary of Interior Fred Seaton agreed to some modifications of the Termination Policy, but many Indians remained dissatisfied.

Congress provided for termination proceedings to take place on a piecemeal basis for Indian rancheros in Southern California.

The Alaska Statehood Act in Section 4 clearly recognized natives' rights -- but Section 6 (b) authorized the new state to select 102,550,000 acres from the public land within twenty-five years! Native Indians' rights were jeopardized because the definition of Alaskan natives was not provided.

In January the actions of the Lumbees of North Carolina captured the admiration of Americans when they emerged from obscurity to drive hooded Ku Klux Klansmen off their lands with shotguns. Finally, the Indians could no longer endure sending their children 35 miles each way to a state-run Indian school. For six years the Lumbees had asked for an Indian school closer to their homes in Harnett County. The KKK had been attempting to intimidate them, but had not counted on limitations to the Lumbees' patience.

1959 Maria Martinez (Maria the Potter) of San Ildefonso Pueblo in New Mexico was awarded the Jane Addams Award by Rockford College, one of the highest honors ever granted to an American woman.

Under Public Law 86-121, Congress authorized the Surgeon General to construct or otherwise provide and maintain essential sanitation facilities for Indian homes, communities and lands.

The Department of the Interior announced that it would no longer object to trust conveyances of land. The decision came after an argument with the pueblo of Santo Domingo (N.M.), which took the position that it would not accept a particular tract of land unless it was conveyed in trust status.

1960 The first secondary level education program in an Alaskan B.I.A. day school was established with the installation of the 9th grade at Uhalakleet.

The U.S. Census showed approximately 509,000 Indians, plus some 43,000 "Alaskan Natives" -- identified as 14,500 Indians and 28,600 Aleuts and Eskimos. In that census, a self-enumeration technique was employed for the first time which allowed the reporting individual to identify his racial origin. Of the ones residing outside of Alaska, 453,000 were found to be in 23 Federal Indian Reservation states, and 56,100 in the remaining 25 states and the District of Columbia.

After years of negotiations, a long step toward solution of the Meccosubee Seminole land problem was taken on October 5, when the Interior Department and the State of Florida agreed on joint use of land that would secure for this unconquered people the use and occupancy of their homeland. Florida assigned 200,000 acres of Indian Trust land to the U.S. for administration and development for the Indians.

When two brothers, Eugene and James Chance, Lumbees of North Carolina, persisted in their attempt to enroll their children in Dunn High School, they were fined $150 and $100 respectively for "aiding, abetting and encouraging their children" to attend school in defiance of a court order. They were not protesting triple segregation (separate Negro, White and Indian schools), but the refusal of the school board to build a school closer than one requiring daily 73 mile round trips for their children.

1961   Secretary of Interior Udall named a Task Force on Indian Affairs, which was scheduled to report back later that year with a report of long-range recommendations.

The American Indian Conference in Chicago, composed of 460 representatives of 90 tribal groups, declared, "It would be well if all our children would avail themselves of academic training." A more detailed set of specifications set forth goals such as adequate training, and counseling and guidance opportunities, Improved housing and better medical facilities, employment, revolving loan funds, industrial development of the reservations, and other allied items of a decent way of living in the 20th century.

Secretary of Interior Stewart Udall launched a study of Indian rights in the State of Washington after approximately 35 Indian groups complained of a variety of encroachments of Indian rights and lands.

Philleo Nash was appointed Commissioner of Indian Affairs.

A National Indian Youth Council activist group was formed in protest against traditional approaches of the older organizations.

A report on education showed that the number of young Indians from the reservations who entered college during the period 1950 to 1960 went from 6,599 to 17,000; and the number of high school students more than doubled from 24,000 to 57,000.

1962   Analysis of reports of BIA assistance to enterprises for eco-
        nomic development during the past year showed that 12 new
        ventures were offered aid, all but two of them in the western
        part of the nation.

        On May 24 Haskell Institute in Lawrence, Kansas (founded in
        1884) was dedicated as a Registered National Historical Land-
        mark.

1963   Annie Dodge Wauneka, a Navajo, was awarded the Medal of
        Freedom Award by President Kennedy a few days before his
        assassination. This award is the highest peace-time honor, and
        is given to persons who have made outstanding contributions to
        the national interest or security, to world peace, or who have
        otherwise made substantial contributions in public or private
        endeavors.

        Horzi Nez (Tall Cliff Dweller) was the name given by the Navajos
        to Oliver La Farge, eloquent spokesman for the Indians, writer,
        historian, anthropologist and long-time president of the Asso-
        ciation on American Indian Affairs, who died on August 2. He
        helped many tribes and individuals in their struggle for self-
        reliance. He was winner of the Pulitzer Prize for fiction in
        1930 for his novel, Laughing Boy, a Navajo love story.

        Commissioner of Indian Affairs, Dr. Philleo Nash said, "Today,
        after a century and a half of program responsibilities by the
        Bureau of Indian Affairs, American Indians on the reservations
        and near the reservations, receive an income between one-
        quarter and one-third of the national average; have about four
        and a half times the unemployment; have an educational level
        about one-half that of the country as a whole, and have a life
        expectancy about two-thirds that of the rest of the country."

        The Alaska Native Business Credit Fund was created by the Asso-
        ciation of American Indian Affairs as a pilot project to enable
        individual Eskimos and Indians to start small businesses.

        The American Indian Arts Center opened in December at 843
        Lexington Avenue in New York City. Its purpose was to develop
        a broader market for the wealth of Indian and Eskimo crafts-
        manship and to give evidence to the public of the high standards
        of Indian workmanship and excellence of American indigenous
        art. In a few months the initial thirty-five tribes that contrib-
        uted had grown to over fifty.

The growing aspiration of young Indians, plus increased Congressional appropriations, permitted granting 963 awards for scholarship aid to attend college during this year.

1964　　　The average American Indian family had an annual income of $1,500 in 1962, or one-half of the $3,000 figure considered to be the national poverty line, according to Dr. Leopna Baumgartner, Assistant Secretary of State.

On November 3, the Sioux of North Dakota scored the greatest political victory in Indian history and retained the right to police their reservations. They won with the solid backing of fellow Dakotans. The voters of North Dakota rejected a law that would have extended state civil and criminal jurisdiction to the Indian reservations. The final referendum was defeated by a four-to-one margin. This was the culmination of nineteen months of hard work, when the people rejected powerful ranching interests aimed at taking over large areas of valuable Indian land.

1965　　　In September the Indian Claims Commission ruled that the Blue Lake area of Carson National Park in New Mexico had been taken illegally and unfairly from the Taos Pueblo. It awarded a monetary judgment, but the Indians refused to accept the dollars, asking Congress to return their religious sanctuary. U.S. Senator Clinton Anderson proposed Senate Bill 3085 to accomplish this objective, but it died without action when Congress adjourned.

1966　　　In a mid-April conference, Secretary of the Interior Stewart L. Udall called for "foundation legislation" to give more elasticity to the trusteeship responsibility for Indian lands and to enable the Indian people to accelerate economic development of their resources.

On April 27, at White House ceremonies to swear in Robert L. Bennett as Commissioner, President Lyndon B. Johnson said: "...The time has come to put the first Americans first on our agenda. From this hour forward we are going to look to you to discharge that responsibility. I want...to begin work today on the most comprehensive program for the advancement of the Indians that the Government of the United States has ever considered...."

On May 31 President Johnson signed into law a five-year $250,000 trachoma contact program for Indians. Another $100,000 pilot program was for mental health in Alaska. It came as a result of a 1964 finding that 7,043 cases of trachoma had been reported--

a 124 percent increase over 1963 . In some southwestern Indian schools as many as 63 percent of the children were reported infected .

The total gross value received from agricultural production on Indian reservations was approximately $170 million . This included crop production, livestock production and direct use of fish and wildlife by Indians . Gross production provided Indian operators $58.6 million .

On November 3, a $10 million housing program planned to ease the substandard housing of 43,000 Eskimos, Indian and Aleut citizens of Alaska living in more than 200 villages became law .

Public Health Service report showed drastic improvement in health of Indians . Random selections included a drop of 61 percent from 1954 in the death rate from tuberculosis for Indians; and for the Alaskan natives, it dropped from 236 to 18 in 1964 . (These appeared to resemble the general national rates of fifteen years ago .) The number of deaths of Indian babies showed a sharp decline of 45 percent between 1954 and 1964, although the Indian infant death rate is still 1-1/2 times higher than that of the general American population .

150,000 Indian children in the age bracket 6-18 enrolled in 216 Bureau of Indian Affairs schools in the United States .

1966   In December, the BIA signed a contract with the Radio Corporation of America to establish the first "family-centered" residential training opportunity center, which is operated at Philadelphia, Mississippi, adjacent to the Choctaw Reservation. Many "families" have since completed training and are employed as a result of this venture which is aimed at the "whole family."

1967   On November 7, 1st Sgt. Pascal Cleatur Poolaw was killed in action . This Indian's family's service deserves more than passing notation . 1st Sgt. Poolaw had been a veteran of three wars, when his end came in a hero's death in Vietnam . Four other sons also served there -- one losing a leg in an encounter with the Viet Cong. After recovery from the treatments at Brooke Army Hospital, Pascal Poolaw, Jr., despite the loss of his leg, requested retention in service and a return to the Vietnam fighting front!

The American Indian Historical Society opposed the segregated school plan, RETS, operated by a private firm with government funds in Oakland, California.

A new junior college in the East Bay Area of California was named Ohlone College, in honor of a now virtually extinct Indian group that formerly lived on land now used by the school.

The White Mountain Apache Tribe of Arizona dedicated a new $350,000 Municipal Center and Council Hall in July.

Federal agencies, other than the Bureau of Indian Affairs, spent more than $193 million on various programs from which Indians received direct benefits.

Mrs. Ramona Zephier of Flandreau, South Dakota, an enrolled member of the Cheyenne River Sioux Tribe, was among the ten finalists in the Mrs. America contest in San Diego. Mrs. Zephier said she regarded the trip to California as an opportunity to "destroy some stereotypes" about how the Indian lives and works. "I don't go for sit-ins," she said, "and I don't presume to speak for the Indian people, but maybe this will show Indians that they can do anything if they really want to do it." The Sioux beauty received her bachelor's degree in home economics from South Dakota State University and does substitute teaching at Flandreau.

1968   On January 22, President Lyndon Johnson spoke to the Navajo Tribe by telephone during ceremonies marking the opening of the 100th anniversary of the signing of the Treaty of 1868 with the United States.

On January 25, the U.S. Indian Claims Commission attempted to award the Mescalero Apaches of New Mexico $8.5 million as compensation for land taken by the United States in the 19th century. This action was heard by the House of Representatives Indian Affairs Subcommittee. They learned that the Mescalero elders refused the money because U.S. law forbade them to split the proceeds with the Lipan and Chiricahua branches of the Apache tribes. The House committee decided to present a bill to allow the three branches to combine present and future proceeds from the government. It was planned that the proceeds would be used for a massive program of investments and social improvement projects.

Public Law 90-252 approved on February 3, authorized an increase of Indian adult vocational education expenditures from $15,000,000 to $25,000,000.

The 1967 Fiscal Report of the Navajo Tribe of Arizona, issued on February 9, showed that the Indians had contracted a white man's habit and were governing by deficit spending, according to Chairman Raymond Nakai. The Chairman pointed out that deficit spending, which started several years ago, was continuing. Earnings in the year totaled $13 million, with $22 million spent. A significant item of the report showed that the tribe had $10 million in a scholarship fund for Navajo students. The interest earnings on the fund totaled $700,000 in the fiscal year 1967.

Latest reports on Navajo children showed that more than 90 percent, or more than 46,000 between the ages of 6 and 18 years, were in school. The dramatic finding of the report is that more than 70 percent of those in school were now finishing high school, closely approximating the national average.

The Bureau of Indian Affairs' latest information reveals that it operates 226 schools, with an enrollment of 51,595 Indian children, and 18 dormitories for 4,204 children attending public schools.

A June report of employment practices by Roman Catholic priest Fr. Justus Wirth of the Zuni, New Mexico area, raised some thought-provoking points regarding the employment of women rather than men by new industries moving onto Indian reservations. He refuted claims that men were irresponsible and undependable. He felt that jobs were needed for Indian men, not women, and that actually the present trend was failing Indian men.

"Project Own", launched by the Small Business Administration and assisted by the Service Corps of Retired Executives, was represented by BIA Assistant Commissioner for Economic Development George Hubley as a tremendous opportunity for Indians to open their own service businesses on their own reservations, filling basic needs for laundromats, gas stations, etc. Loan money in this historic revolution resulted from changing attitudes and willingness of the banking institutions to look at minority requests for business aid more from the basis of character than from the normal criterion of collateral. The SBA will guarantee independent ventures including franchises, but

but not manufacturing enterprises, up to 90 percent of such loans to $350,000. However, in localities where unemployment is chronically very high, SBA may fully guarantee loans up to $25,000. With loans being made through banks rather than the SBA, credit and character checks become more personalized and realistic.

Navajo Community College, at Many Farms, Chinle, Arizona, opened in the fall on the big reservation, thereby becoming a first in Indian colleges. This culminated the long-standing dream of many Navajo leaders to provide higher education right on the reservation. (Bacone College in Oklahoma was for a long time an all-Indian two year school operated by the Baptist Home Missionary Society, but it is no longer exclusively operated for Indians.)

Approximately 200,000 Indians moved to urban areas in the past decade, some with financial help from the federal government. The exact figure is difficult to come by, because the Indian is free to move about as he pleases.

On September 7, the Reverend Dr. Roe B. Lewis of Phoenix, Arizona, of Pima and Papago blood, was named to receive the 1968 Indian Achievement Award presented annually by the Indian Council Fire. The award was established in 1933 at the Century of Progress Exposition. The Presbyterian minister was chosen because of his outstanding service in educational counselling work for the Indians, and for assisting Indian high school graduates through college and graduate school.

In an October Special Report on Economic Development, the BIA's Indian Record cited that 10,000 new jobs had been created in Indian communities since 1962, as a direct result of efforts by combined forces of BIA and tribal groups. The fact that 4,000 Indians were hired was a cheerful notation.

In a December report, the Indian Claims Commission showed that since its inception in 1946, it had completed action on 125 dockets involving 103 awards totaling $279,549,641.00. Another 136 cases were dismissed. Still pending are 343 dockets. Fortunately, Congress had extended the life of this important body just before its scheduled demise and provided for two more judges in an attempt to speed up results on the remaining cases.

As the year ended, the Nation's largest non-federal employer of Indians, Fairchild Semi-Conductor Corporation, announced intentions to add another 500 workers to its production crew at Shiprock, New Mexico, thereby making a total work force of 1,200. The firm had been operating in a temporary building leased from the Navajo Tribe for over a year, and commenced construction on a new and larger building in December.

1969   In January, final inspection was made of the main canal and Tunnel #2 of the large Navajo Irrigation Project, designed to supply long-awaited water in Arizona to irrigate arid soils for the Indians. That phase of the project had a construction cost of about $9 million, of which $2,750,000 wnet for payments to the workers.

Sixteen percent of the professional teaching staff of the Bureau of Indian Affairs were Indians.

In April the Cochiti Pueblo in New Mexico signed a 99-year lease with Great Western United Corporation for 7,500 acres of land adjacent to the Cochiti Lake and Dam being created by the U.S. Army Corps of Engineers. The act was a tremendous departure from past practices of whites desirous of using Indian lands. Construction of thousands of resort-type homes and other recreational facilities were planned on this site, located 35 miles from Albuquerque. It was hailed as a major step in improving the economic independence of Indians, but not only was there to be income from the land, but the Indians were to be trained and employed wherever possible in this venture.

PFC Joseph Michael Mermejo from Picuris Pueblo in New Mexico became the first member of his pueblo to die in the war in Vietnam. The 19 year old Marine was killed near Que Nam on March 29 and had been in the theatre since October, 1968.

Dr. N. Scott Momaday, 34-year-old Kiowa Indian, was awarded the Pulitzer Prize for literature in May, and became the first member of his race to be given the coveted recognition for his book House Made of Dawn, a novel about the tribulations of an Indian Veteran of World War II.

A May report by BIA Commissioner Robert L. Bennett revealed that fifty percent of the total Indian population was under the age of 17 years.

"Nok-A-Homa," the Atlanta Brave's mascot, was burned out of his teepee in May when one of his smoke bombs backfired. Levi Walker, an Ottawa-Chippewa Indian from Charlevoix, Michigan, camped out behind the left field fence in the Atlanta Stadium. During the regular baseball season, he set off smoke bombs and went into a war dance to celebrate every Brave homerun.

Robert L. Bennett, Indian Commissioner, resigned on May 31, concluding one of the longest tenures in office. He was only the second Indian to hold that significant post.

After analyzing the historical decline of educational attainment by Indian groups, principally that of the Choctaws and the Cherokee Republics, after the white man took control, a June report of the influential Carnegie Corporation suggested that BIA educational officials be rewarded according to the degree that they managed to involve the Indian community in making decisions at the top levels, and that some of the Bureau's responsibilities should be transferred to the communities. Possibly the most significant proposal was the creation of a federal commission for Indian education, limited to a five-year period, with the understanding that thereafter it would return control to Indian communities. In its composition there would be officials from the BIA, the U.S. Office of Education, tribal groups, etc. The Commission would be charged with the duty of training Indians for administering and staffing Indian schools and providing consultant support to Indian school boards as they emerged and asked for help. Further, it would supply necessary funds to revise curricula to a pragmatic reflection of the true history, culture and values of the Indian. In their conclusion, the investigators in effect found that education could not get any worse under control of the Indians, and the possibilities for improvement were tremendous.

Janet Sanborn, an eighteen year old Bangor, Maine, high school graduate, worked during the summer as a volunteer at the Sanostee Boarding School of the Bureau of Indian Affairs. The "guest worker" program allows individuals to donate their services to the BIA. Miss Sanborn was the first such volunteer in the Shiprock, N.M., area, which serves the Navajo people. She paid her own way (transportation and expenses) and showed a love for humanity in working with the mental retardation project.

In July, Miss Margery Haury, 18, a Navajo-Sioux-Arapahoe-Cheyenne, won the title of Miss Indian America XVI at Sheridan,

Wyoming. She was a political science student at the University of New Mexico in Albuquerque, planning to go into law. Commenting on the importance of teaching pride in heritage, she said, "I would like to engender a closeness between all tribes. Most of the other minorities have a common goal. We don't. We're all so different, yet we must unite."

In August, Indian leaders from 36 tribes strongly opposed the policy of termination which they claimed was threatening their lands and rights. The loosely knit Indian Task Force took exception to statements of Interior Secretary Walter Hickel that American Indians were overprotected and were using the trust status of the reservation lands to perpetuate their dependency.

On August 7, after vainly urging for a timely appointment of a new Commissioner of Indian Affairs for eight months, the Indians were advised that President Nixon and Secretary of the Interior Walter Hickel had settled on Louis R . Bruce, a Mohawk-Oglala-Sioux blooded Indian from New York. Bruce thereby became the third Indian in history to assume the high governmental post. Before him were his immediate predecessor, Robert L . Bennett, and General Ely Samuel Parker, who served during President Grant's administration. Bruce, although surrounded by a luxurious New York atmosphere, did maintain contacts with his people. His father was a Mohawk Indian and a doctor by profession, and his Oglala Sioux mother came from the Pine Ridge Reservation in South Dakota. The new commissioner grew up on the New York State St . Regis Mohawk Reservation. He is a graduate of Cazenovia Seminary and Syracuse University. He organized the first National Indian Conference on Housing in 1961, and earlier he was New York State Director for Indian projects in the National Youth Administration. He was formerly a dairy farmer and still owns a dairy farm in New York. He served as the executive secretary of the National Congress of American Indians, and was awarded the American Indian Achievement Award and the Freedoms Award, among other honors.

On August 27, four youngsters from the Pala Mission School in California were honored guests on the nationally televised Art Linkletter Show. During the show, the famous entertainer told the audience, "This is the first time Indian children have ever appeared on my show."

On August 29, the Interior Department announced that it had renewed its contract with Thiokol Chemical Corp. for the operation of its Indian job training center at Roswell, New Mexico. The cost of operations for 1970 was $2,289,850. The Indians are brought to the Thiokol operation by the BIA as whole families, thus avoiding one of the problems which plagued prior Indian training endeavors, drop-outs by homesick students. The whole family is exposed to programs designed to make the Indians not only technically more proficient, but also to equip them with understanding for living in the mainstream of 21st century America. Wives receive nutritional home economics assistance, and children are taken care of in nurseries while the parents are away. The older children attend the regular Roswell schools. Unemployed and under-employed Indians are reported to be very enthusiastic with their new opportunities to learn "in-depth" the technical and living skills to which they are being exposed.

An Employment Training Center for Indians from the northern plains states opened at Bismarck, N.D., in September, by a corporation composed of the Indian tribes of North Dakota. The United Tribes of North Dakota Development Corporation became the first center initiated by Indians and having an Indian contractor. Initial enrollment was composed of 25 families, 10 solo parents, 50 single men and 50 single women. Because wives often took training too, a total of 160 people entered into the actual training program, funded from several federal sources.

A September follow-up of Indian high school graduates in the Southwest in 1962 indicated that almost three-fourths of those contacted continued their education. More than two-thirds of those who went on completed their programs, a majority in vocational-technical subjects. However, only seven percent completed college, while 44 percent finished vocational training programs. A significant finding was that an overwhelming majority of the respondents thought it important to speak in the tribal language. Of extreme importance was the claim by more than nine out of ten of the graduates that they had never experienced prejudice in high school.

National names and top political figures joined the Navajos in dedicating the largest industrial factory in the State of New Mexico at Shiprock on September 6. Included were David and Julie Eisenhower, Senator Joseph Montoya, newly appointed Indian commissioner Louis R. Bruce, a Mohawk, and New Mexico Governor David Cargo. Fairchild Semiconductors, a subsidiary of world-wide Fairchild Camera and Instrument Corporation, is engaged in assembling some of the components for the Apollo rocket systems. From its modest beginning, when only 50 workers were employed, it has grown to a plant employing 1,200, including more Indian people than any other plant of any kind in the entire United States. Less than thirty key employes are not Indians. The firm is a joint partnership involving private industry, tribal authorities, federal aid agencies and the larger New Mexico community. It succeeded because the Navajos believed in themselves and convinced others that their belief was well founded. Navajo Fairchild hopes to double and triple the current payroll in the near future and convert all jobs to Indian occupancy as quickly as Indian skills can be trained to assume the entire range of responsibilities.

In September, Paddy Martinez, the Navajo sheepherder who picked up a yellow rock on Haystack Mountain and started New Mexico's multi-million dollar uranium industry, died in a Grants hospital at the age of 78. Although his discovery of uranium brought riches to many, Paddy lived in a simple hogan near the shores of Bluewater Lake, grazing sheep. His strike was on property owned by the Santa Fe Railway. The railway rewarded him by giving him a life-time pension.

On September 15, the Senate Interior Subcommittee, prodded by U.S. Senator Joseph M. Montoya, agreed to a $2 million increase in the $3.5 million budget request of the Nixon Administration for the Navajo Indian Irrigation Project. The committee found the lower figure totally inadequate. The project, which was to be completed in 1979, is already tragically behind schedule, and at the delayed rate of appropriations, skyrocketing construction costs now threaten to double if it is not completed until 1990 or later. When completed, the project will provide irrigation for 110,000 acres of land and create 1,120 new farm jobs for Navajo families, while additionally creating sufficient new jobs and economic activity for up to 80,000 Navajos.

On September 24, the Commissioner of Indian Affairs reported that Indian timber income in the United States amounted to $32.7 million -- twice the amount of two years ago from sales of reservation lumber in fiscal year 1969. Indian tree resources are harvested on a sustained-yield basis, to prevent over-cutting and eventual depletion. The Bureau official estimated that the present allowable harvest of 1.04 billion board feet may be reached in fiscal year 1970. Just as important as the income from timber sales are the job opportunities in lumbering and lumber processing created by the harvest. At the present rate, 7,000 full-time jobs are directly related with an additional 4,000 in supporting and service employment. Commissioner Louis R. Bruce pointed out that several tribes are taking increased interest in developing their resources and that about 30 percent of the total volume of Indian timber is purchased by Indian and tribal enterprises.

On October 1, Indian parents in Ridgeville, South Carolina, turned away when confronted by a line of federal marshals, and threatened with contempt of court charges at a school where they sought to enroll their children. They wanted the children sent to desegregated schools where they believed they would get a better education. "If it takes this to get my children into the Ridgeville school, then I die," said Mrs. Gertie Creel, the mother of an eight year old who lives in the small Indian settlement in rural Dorchester County. The Indians and their Negro civil rights backers vowed to continue a drive to close small county Indian schools. The federal judge's order prohibited disturbances at the school.

Groundbreaking ceremonies for the new $8 million Albuquerque Vocational Technical School for Indians were held on October 5, 1969. Remarks were delivered by Domingo Montoya, Chairman of the All Indian Pueblo Council, U.S. Senator Clinton P. Anderson, Louis R. Bruce, Commissioner of Indian Affairs, and others. The inclusion of representatives from Indian youth was significant, for it was revealed that 65 percent of the Indians are under the age of 25 years. Commissioner Bruce commented that he hadn't been able to get to church in the morning, but had sat there meditating in the balmy autumn sunshine of New Mexico, with an intensely blue, cloudless sky and the vista of the breathtaking Sandia Mountains in front of him and the ancient volcanos to his back. "What a beautiful chapel the Great Spirit has given us here," he added, unaware that the ground had once been the site of the now vanished Alameda Indians. The school is unique in that Indians have been represented in all the planning and actions taken in the past, and will continue to be as they teach and administer in the new plant. The educational complex will not school merely post-high school youth, but will house them in happy surroundings as they prepare for life and vocation in sub-professional endeavors. The new plant is so designed to attract students from all over the United States, and was designed first by considering the curriculum needs of the future and the pupils who would be attending, and then by building the plant around such requirements. It will be a place to which the Indian can return when he feels the need to up-date or up-grade his skills. It will be available to married students and those who are employed, but who can obtain additional education by utilizing the plant in the evenings and on weekends, thus effecting a break-through in cost-saving in Indian educational needs. An initial 500 students will open the multi-million dollar school, with an additional 1,000 students in years subsequent to the fall of 1971.

American Indians from all parts of the United States, ranging from Seminoles of Florida to Yakimas of Washington, and many interested whites, flocked to Albuquerque, New Mexico, for the opening of the annual five-day convention of the National Congress of American Indians on October 6, 1969. Political figures, office holders and Indian beauties (including Miss Indian America who happened to come from Albuquerque) high-lighted the event, which featured a colorful parade of almost sixty floats and included tribal dancers, Indian bands and the governors of many pueblos. Featured speakers were the Secretary of the Interior Walter Hickel and the Commissioner of Indian Affairs Louis R. Bruce.

At the opening of the 26th annual convention in Albuquerque, New Mexico, on October 6, Wendell Chino, president of the National Congress of American Indians, said that the American Indian is disappointed and frustrated, but not beaten down. "There are lots of times when the federal government doesn't fulfill its obligation to the Indian people, " he stated, before his keynote address. In his evening address to some 1,000 delegates, he came out strongly against White House plans for channeling Indian funds through states, saying, "It would put us all out in the cold. Federal assistance must be granted to Indian tribes in the same way it is granted to states for their uses -- directly."

On Tuesday, October 7, U.S. Senator Edward Kennedy called for a White House conference on Indian problems as a giant step for initiating rapid major improvements for Indians. He said that he would introduce a bill to authorize and finance such a project. At the same time he criticized the Bureau of Interior's handling of Indian Affairs as "unsatisfactory even under the best of circumstances." Calling for the creation of a Select Committee on Human Needs of American Indians, the Senator said, "The BIA is notorious for its resistance to reform, to innovation, and to discharging its responsibilities in a competent and sensitive fashion."

On October 7, Michael Benson, 18, a Navajo college student, claimed that Navajo Elders ignore youth and should express more confidence in them. Stating his views during a youth panel at the National Indian Congress meetings, he said, "Many Indian youth are disappointed in our leaders. They don't talk to us much." Benson, president of the Native American Students, which is composed of Indian students attending eastern preparatory schools and colleges, was applauded by some 400 listeners. At the same panel, Lehman Brightman of Berkeley, California, head of an Indian group called the "United Native Americans," circulated a petition calling for the removal from office of Interior Secretary Walter Hickel. To the panel audience he said, "Hickel is the greatest enemy of the American Indian and we should get rid of such a menace. Our present Indian leadership has dwindled to talkers and rubber stamps of what the Bureau Of Indian Affairs puts in front of them." He concluded that Indians are led around by the nose by white people,and Indian supporters of the BIA are "Uncle Tomahawks." Outside the hotel where the meetings were in progress, a number of Indian young people carried placards calling for the removal of Hickel, but said that they were not connencted with any special group.

On October 8, Vice-President Spiro Agnew promised the American Indians that the Nixon administration would not adopt a termination policy to phase out federal supervision of Indian Affairs. He claimed that the President would work with them on a "community-by-community and tribe-by-tribe basis " Possibly warning of a future turn of events, however, he said that the national administration will "urge greater local leadership on the part of the Indian."

Secretary of the Interior Walter Hickel on October 8 followed up the Vice President's remarks to the Congress of American Indians, saying, "With your ideas and your trust we can make words come to life. I can help. But in the final analysis the future of the Indians -- America's first citizens -- must be shaped by the Indians." He praised the new Indian Commissioner saying, "Bruce has my support and my ear."

In October, Navajo Tribal Chairman Raymond Nakai signed a lease agreement for the construction of a $309 million electric generating plant to be built at Page, Arizona. Coal royalties, lease payments and other contributions from the operation will exceed $1,8 million annually for the Hopi and Navajo tribes.

In October, the Office of Economic Opportunity announced continued support for the Navajo Community College which opened
in January at Many Farms, Arizona. It is the first college in
the country to be planned, developed and operated by and for
Indians. In awarding the grant, the OEO said that it is supporting this unique attempt to prove that a college can be responsive to educational and economic needs of a rural community. The college serves as a laboratory for experimenta-
tion in the field of Indian education. It enrolls promising high-
risk youths and under-educated adults. Ned Hatathli, a Navajo,
is President.

AMERIND, an organization founded to protect the rights and
improve the working conditions of Indian employees, opened in
late October, with Headquarters at 3102 Central Avenue, S.W.,
Albuquerque, New Mexico. The organization, according to
Doug Sakiestewa, National Indian Youth Council member, evolved
from the experiences of some Indian employees of the BIA who
filed discrimination complaints in Albuquerque and Gallup. Mr.
Sakiestewa stated that the organization is designed to fight employment discrimination and end the "second class treatment"
of Indians working for the BIA, U.S. Public Health Service and
other federal agencies serving Indian people. There are no dues
or membership applications required for joining in the purposes
and objectives of the new group. Financing of initial expenses
will be borne by the NIYC.

1970   With the advent of the New Year, Indian and white groups were
concerned at the abysmally low economic place which the Indian
had in an otherwise healthy and vigorous national picture. Indian youth groups pressed for change, agitating for a "new look"
for the "First Americans" through the use of political power
accomplished with activism, previously held to be unacceptable
Indian conduct by the elder, conservative Indians.

On January 1, the California Indian tribes of the San Diego area
completed a proposal under the auspices of the Wright Institute
at Grossmont College to the government in Washington. They
requested financing for a research and development program to
uncover and implement solutions for minority and low income
peoples in that area. Participating in the program were members of the ad hoc committee representing Indians, students,
administrators and faculty of three community colleges of the
area -- Grossmont, Mesa and Palomar. The program followed
meetings and questionnaires which ascertained the problems
and needs of local Indian peoples and of the areas in which they

live. The proposal was sent to the Special Services Office in
the Office of Health, Education and Welfare. Implementation
date was targeted for September, 1970. Conference leaders
indicated there were federal funds available for such a purpose.

In February the "Indians of All Tribes," issued a statement
calling for renewed support of their November 1969 occupation of Alcatraz Island. They continued to base their claim
to ownership upon an old U.S. statute regarding abandonment
of lands. While disclaiming to speak for all Indians, they
proposed plans for the use of the former federal penitentiary
which would benefit all Indians.

March 5. Vine Deloria, Jr. (Sioux) made a plea supporting
the efforts of the Indians who had occupied Alcatraz Island
in an effort to have that no longer used facility given to them
for office centers which would concentrate upon Indian problems, today and tomorrow. Admitting that some people might
object to that concept, he dramatically pointed out that the
Health, Education and Welfare Department had given out 10
million dollars in 1969 to non-Indians to study Indians, but
had not appropriated a single dollar to an Indian scholar or
researcher to show the views of Indians.

The first Convocation of American Indian Scholars convened
at Princeton University, from March 23-26, under the chairmanship of Dr. Alfonso Ortiz, a San Juan Pueblo Indian. The
meeting was held under the auspices of the American Indian
Historical Society with the purpose of bringing together Indian
students.

A research and development office for a Native American
Centre for Living Arts was opened in March in New York
City. The project was conceived by the internationally known
Cree folk singer, Buffy Sainte Marie.

On April 17, the Tesuque Pueblo Governor signed a ninety-
nine-year lease with Santos E. Campos and the Sangre de
Cristo Development Co. for 5400 acres of pueblo land for
the creation of a resort city north of Santa Fe, New Mexico,
which was to provide income and jobs for tribal members.

In his message to the Congress of the United States on New Policies and Goals for American Indians on July 8, 1970, President Richard Nixon presented a new Indian Doctrine. Acknowledging that the story of the Indian in America was a sorry one indeed, he stated "it is long past time that Indian policies of the Federal government began to recognize and build upon the capacities and insights of the Indian people. Both as a matter of justice and as a matter of enlightened social policy, we must begin to act on the basis of what the Indians themselves have long been telling us." Among the highlights and promises Nixon made were: Self-determination without termination; Indians to direct the programs; Restoration of Blue Lake to the Taos Pueblo; Local school control; Economic development legislation; More money for Indian health; Helping urban Indians; The establishment of an Indian Trust Counsel Authority to assure the independent legal representation for Indian natural resource rights; and The establishment of a new position in the Department of the Interior -- Assistant Secretary for Indian and Territorial Affairs.

In July Commissioner of Indian Affairs Bruce signed a contract with the Ramah Navajo School Board to provide $368,000 a year for the next three years. The people of Ramah started their own high school which they planned to organize and operate themselves with federal funds provided.

On July 31 the U.S. Congress ruled that a new roll must be prepared of those Indians who are lineage descendants of the Weas, Piankashaws, Peorias and Kaskaskias tribes, who were parties to the Treaty of May 30, 1854, so that certain living descendents of those tribes could share more than $2 million.

In August the Ford Foundation announced that the California Indian Legal Service had been awarded a grant to establish a nationwide demonstration program to engage in major litigation involving Indian rights. Known as the Native American Rights Fund, the staff included John E. Echohawk, a recent graduate of the University of New Mexico Law School. The Foundation grant of $155,000 was for an eighteen month operation and to fund major litigation of widespread concern to many Indians, including cases involving water rights, land claims, fighting and hunting rights, health, sanitation and education.

A five-day seminar during the week of August 10 started the first national gathering of American Indian women ever to be held. Meeting at Fort Collins, Colorado, sixty-eight women from Indian communities from Alaska to Florida sought to determine how they could help people back home meet the wide variety of challenges of the 1970s. The group chose Mrs. James M. (Marie) Cox, a Comanche from Midwest, Oklahoma, as executive director for the new group.

The most significant development since the filing of the San Luis Rey water case occured in September when Interior Secretary Walter J. Hickel, acting as trustee for the Rincon, La Jolla and San Pascual bands of Mission Indians, filed a petition with the Federal Power Commission to revoke the license of the Escondido Mutual Water Company. The petition claimed that the company was in violation of its license when it constructed a diversion dam across the San Luis Rey river on the La Jolla Reservation; that it had trespassed on the La Jolla, Rincon and San Pascual Indian reservations without authority; and that the water company had failed to provide water to the Indians in accordance with its agreement. At stake were water rights of the Mission Indian bands and millions of dollars of past damage.

September 8. The Ramah Chapter of the Navajo Indian Reservation witnessed the culmination of their dreams (1) to form a school board independent of the regular New Mexico State Department of Education and the BIA; and (2) to open their own junior/senior high school. They had sought for two years to resolve the state ordered closing of an old school with their children then having to attend BIA boarding schools or travel to Zuni, forty miles away. Many battles later and arguments ended, the new school opened with the real focus of the program bringing Indians -- students, parents and Board members -- together to discuss what was important in terms of a Navajo education. The consensus was that "on graduation the students should be able to understand and participate in Navajo culture, be employable and able to go to college if they chose." Navajo was then to be an integral part of the curriculum. The school was funded by other than state resources and open to all resident students regardless of racial background.

September 18. A suit in behalf of treaty fishing rights of Indian tribes in the State of Washington was filed by the Department of Justice at the request of the Department of Interior. The suit was similar to one filed two years ago in Oregon. The Oregon case did much to clarify Indian fishing rights on the Columbia River. Secretary Hickel said, "We hope this suit will have the same effect on fishing rights in the Puget Sound and Olympic Peninsula area of the state of Washington." The action was brought on behalf of seven tribes: the Payallup, Nisqually, Skokomish, Makah, Quileute, Hoh and Muckleshoot.

September 19. Laguna pueblo, the youngest Indian pueblo in New Mexico with but 273 years behind it, presented its annual fiesta and harvest dance. The history of the Lagunas dates back to 1697 when Indians from a number of scattered pueblos gathered there and established a pueblo of their own. The site they picked was on a rounded, rocky point on the south bank of the San Jose River, in the midst of good grazing land and just east of a lake, or "laguna." The pueblo was formally established in 1699 by Don Pedro de Cubero, governor of New Mexico, on a grant of land given the Indians by the king of Spain. The fiesta is always a colorful affair, with an outdoor market.

October. A small group of concerned organized the New Mexico Council of Indian Women, presumably the first known statewide organization of its kind in the country, according to council president, Mrs. Rita Cortez, Mohawk-Santo Domingo. The purpose of the group was "to demonstrate the dignity and community spirit of the Indian women." "I feel women are a vast untapped human resource and are in direct contact with, or lack of them, in education, health, welfare, human and natural resources," said Mrs. Cortez. "So often men will sit in on meetings, discuss the problems and what should be done and just drop it. We want to see that something is done!"

October. The controversy over awarding controlling interests in a number of businesses and corporations to Indians caused doubts and disturbed friends and foes of such actions which seem to have been caused by contracts obtained through the Buy Indian Act of 1970. In New Mexico and Arizona, there were four firms listing non-Indians as minority stockholders, but with government contracts awarded them through the mechanics of the Act. The act permits non-competitive bidding. Its major requirement is that Indians own more than 50 per cent of the operation.

October 18. Secretary of the Interior Walter J. Hickel announced the appointment of fifteen American Indians to key executive posts in the Washington, D.C., headquarters of the Bureau of Indian Affairs. (The Secretary also named five new BIA officials who were non-Indian.) The appointments were a result of an executive realignment planned earlier in the year to make the BIA more responsive to changing conditions and needs among the Nation's more than 450,000 reservation Indians. The new lines of authority showed two associate commissioners appointed, Harold D. Cox, Creek, native of Tulsa (OK) and Anthony Lincoln, Navajo, Fort Defiance (AZ); and five Indians designated as assistants to the commissioner, Clarence Acoya, a member of the Laguna Indian Pueblo (NM), James Hena, of Tesuque-Zuni Descent (NM), William "Billy" Mills, Sioux, Pine Ridge (SD), Helen Peterson, Oglala Sioux, Pine Ridge (SD), and Harry Rainbolt, a Pima (AZ) native.

October 21. In remarks before the National Congress of American Indians Annual Convention in Anchorage, Alaska, Secretary of the Interior, Walter J. Hickel said, "Together we must launch and sustain a united effort to bring the American Indian to his full stature in American life. Let us set a precedent. Let's fashion together the kind of quality education in which every young Indian not only is prepared to meet the challenges of modern society but understands and is pround of his identity."

As of November 1, the Indian Claims Commission had finished work on 327 of 609 docketts, or sub-petitions of Indian claims, since it was created on August 13, 1946. To date,

Congress has appropriated more than 330 million dollars to Indians as a result of Commission awards. The Commission is a judicial body set up to adjudicate tribal claims against the United States to obtain payment for lands taken from them in the eighteenth and nineteenth centuries.

The world premiere of the new Anthony Quinn movie filmed in Albuquerque, New Mexico, FLAP, benefitted the new Indian studies program of the University of New Mexico on November 19. The proceeds helped establish a student center to serve as a culture and administrative meeting area for the program, with the university providing space and office furniture. The film was shot at many New Mexico pueblos and on the streets of Santa Fe and Albuquerque.

After receiving the bipartisan bill passed by the Senate, President Richard Nixon on December 15 signed the long sought legislation that finally gave the Taos Indians 48,000 acres of land they said was an intrensic part of their religion. The tract, which includes Blue Lake, is nestled high in the Taos Range of the Sangre de Cristo Mountains in New Mexico above the pueblo's present holdings. That ended a sixty-four year fight for the tribe that worships nature. From the fourteenth century on, the Taos have used the lake and the land for tribal and religious purposes. In 1906 the federal government appropriated the land "without compensation," ruled the Indian Claims Commission -- for the creation of Carson National Forest. The effect of the bill is that the title and ownership of the land goes to the Taos, to be held in trust by the Interior Secretary.

1971   In the U.S. Government Fiscal Year, about 43.7 million dollars was spent by the Office of Economic Opportunity, U.S. Office of Education and the Bureau of Indian Affairs for Indian education in public schools. This amounted to about 209 dollars for each Indian pupil. A report into federal funding of Indian education revealed huge discrepancies in the financing of one school to another, and between Indian and non-Indian schools. The report, published by the Bureau of Social Science Research, was authored by Susan Smith and Margaret Walker and undertaken at the request of the Harvard Center for Law and Education, under the Legal

Action Support Project. Amongst other things it showed that on a per capita basis, education in the BIA system costs twice as much as it does in public day schools. Although the report did not deal with the question of benefits gained from the fund, it did note that a disproportionately large amount of BIA school money failed to reach the schools.

Starting this new year off were claims that there were surveillance and investigations of even moderate Indian leaders and their staffs, Indians holding positions in the federal government and Indian community leaders. Indians claimed that the Nixon administration from its first year in office had FBI-gathered information on Indian activity routed in regular intelligence reports to the president's top man for Indian affairs, Leonard Garmet.

January 12. The NAACP Legal Defense and Educational Fund, Inc. charged that federal funds appropriated for the education of Indian children were being used for "every conceivable school need except aiding the 177,000 Indian children in public schools." The charges were based upon a ten month study (of sixty school districts in eight states) investigating the use of 66 million dollars in annual federal aid appropriated for Indian public school students through the 1934 Johnson-O'Malley Act, the impact aid program and Title 1 of the Elementary and Secondary Education Act, providing extra funds for poor children. The NAACP group stated that officials used the funds for "fancy equipment" for white schools and to reduce the taxes of white property owners.

January 14. The U.S. government gave custody of an old Davis, California, Army base to Indians who had occupied the 640 acre site in November 1970. Jack Forbes, a Powhatan Indian, stated that a university for Indians and Mexican-Americans would be developed on the land.

In February, Commissioner of Indian Affairs Louis R. Bruce announced an environmental awareness award program for Indian schools and communities. An outgrowth of the new emphasis upon environment and conservation in

BIA schools, the award program was designed for community-wide involvement. He pointed out that the 219 schools operated by the BIA were stressing environmental awareness through language, arts, social studies, science and art curricula, "in keeping with the National Environmental Policy Act."

In February, the Jicarilla Apache transplanted antelope, buffalo and elk onto their northern New Mexico reservation where world famous trophy-sized mule deer bucks are taken by hunters every year. This project would increase the economy of the tribe from fees charged to non-Indian hunters who journeyed from all over the world to hunt there. Revenue from the sale of hunting and fishing permits is an important source of income and jobs to the Jicarillas.

A Blackfoot Vietnam Veteran, William John Gobert, twenty-nine, was selected Outstanding Handicapped Worker of the Year by the Department of Health, Education and Welfare. The award was presented to him by Mrs. Richard M. Nixon on March 25. He was employed as an instructor by the Indian Health Service in the Community Health Medic Program carried out at the Tucson, Arizona, Desert Willow Training Center.

During April the Economic Development Administration of the U.S. Department of Commerce made twelve grants and one loan for a total outlay of over 6 million dollars to Indian tribes and Indian-related development groups. Assistant Secretary of Commerce Robert A. Podesta released the report which showed that the grants ranged from one of 36,240 dollars to the Cheyenne River Sioux tribe, South Dakota, to one of almost 2 million dollars to the Mescalero Apache tribe of New Mexico.

In a four day White House Conference on Youth held in Estes Park, Colorado, April 18 to 21, the 900 youths aged 14-24 and 500 adults issued a conference report preamble, prepared for presentation to the president which, "Denounced slavery and its evil legacy." Continuing such a line of thought, it stated, "the annihilation of Indians genocide. . . . have undermined the ideals to which the people of this country have aspired."

During a three day Tribal Chairmen's Conference held in Pierre, South Dakota, April 22 to 24, eighteen Indian tribal leaders voted to form the National Tribal Chairmen's Association. The NTCA was formed to make sure federally recognized tribes -- both land based and without -- have proper representation.

The start of a movement among western Indians of the United States "to give the Indians of small tribes a voice equal to the strength exercised presently by the largest Indian tribes in the nation," occured on May 1 in Federal-Way, Washington, at the headquarters of the Small Tribes Organization of Western Washington (STOWW). At the organizational meeting were tribal leaders from California, Nevada, and Washington. "Many of our problems stem from the fact that we (as individual groups and inter-tribal councils) do not have the political clout necessary to enact change on our own," said Roy S. George, Sr., president.

In late May, an innovative public interest law firm, The Institute for the Development of Indian Law, opened its Washington offices in Washington, D.C. President was author-attorney Vine Deloria, and included on the board of directors were such famous Indian leaders as Frank Duchenaux, retired long time Cheyenne River Sioux tribal leader, Robert L. Bennett, Oneida, former commissioner of the Bureau of Indian Affairs and Blair Paul, Tlingit, Seattle attorney. Executive Director Kirke Kickingbird, Kiowa attorney, said that the institute planned to publish a scholarly Indian law journal, to provide a legal information service for tribes and Indian organizations, to prepare in-depth periodic reports on legal aspects of Indian affairs, to litigate in selected cases, to train Indian law students, and to publish a jurisprudence textbook which would contain a total theory of Indian law. It was expected that the institute would work closely with the Indian law program of the University of New Mexico, where Bennett was the director of the Indian Law Center.

Fleming D. Begay, a Navajo Indian, was honored during May by the Bureau of Indian Affairs as "Indian Businessman of the Year." The "Indian Businessman of the Year" award is sponsored by the BIA to honor and encourage Indian businessmen. He is a strong believer in encouraging Indians to get established and do things on their own, but emphasizes that they will need encouragement of the general public.

May 4. The noted anthropology and linguistic professor of American Indians, Dr. Edward P. Dozier, died of a heart attack at his home in Tucson, Arizona. Dr. Dozier was fifty-five years of age and a Santa Clara Indian of international repute.

May 5. Official dedication ceremonies took place for the Kicking Horse Regional Manpower Center -- the country's first all-Indian Job Corps Center -- near Ronan, Montana. Sponsored by the Confederated Salish and Kootenai Tribal Council of the Flathead Reservation, the center was staffed primarily by Indians. Its first group numbered 185 young Indian men ages sixteen to twenty-one, and represented thirty-four Indian tribes and Native Alaskans, from all states west of the Mississippi. All the usual benefits of a Job Corps full resident program were available, plus an Indian cultural enrichment program given by the Indian staff members.

May 14. Residents of the San Carlos Apache Indian reservation (AZ) dedicated their own radio station. Billed as the first and only one on any Indian reservation in the Nation, the San Carlos Community radio station SCCR, 590 KC, broadcasts from 7 A.M. to 5:30 P.M. on a week-day schedule. Operated by locally trained bilingual Indian youths who serve as announcers, newscasters and disc jockeys, it is a unique and versatile closed system that is filling a communication need on the reservation. It operates by using a twenty-five watt carrier transmitter which feeds a signal into already existing 4160 volt power lines, and about ninety per cent of the people can, if they wish, tune in on the SCCR signal.

May 20. James Reger, in testimony to the Montana Water Resources Board in Helena, related how he had maneuvered the Crow Indian tribe leaders to hand over 30,000 acre feet of water a year to coal companies without a penny of payment. The water was needed for gaseficiation plants which were to use coal from the Crow reservation lands bought by the Norsworthy & Reger group for 17.5 cents a ton. (The Crow people only learned about this years later and felt the BIA had, again, not offered them proper protection.)

Included in the May 21 announced selection of sixteen young men and women as White House Fellows was Martin Seneca, a Seneca Indian. The program was designed to provide rising young leaders from businesses, the universities, and a variety of professions a first hand exposure to the top level of the Federal government. Following their year in Washington where their duties were to act as special assistants to members of the White House staff and members of the Cabinet, they return to their respective professions and communities.

May 26. Frank Carlucci, director of the Office of Economic Opportunity (OEO), announced that the federal government would provide 880,000 dollars in various grants to set up a Model Urban Center program, to be administered by OEO and financed by OEO and the Departments of Labor, Housing and Urban Development, and Health, Education and Welfare. The network Indian centers would be located in Los Angeles, Minneapolis, Gallup, New Mexico, and Fairbanks, Alaska, with coordinating offices to be located in New York City. Carlucci indicated that the centers might serve as models to improve services in approximately forty existing urban service centers for Indians.

May 27. In Atlanta, Georgia, in an unusual event the Boy Scouts of America honored Virginia A. Stroud, the 1971 Miss Indian America, by presenting her with a Young American Award for her outstanding accomplishments in the fields of service and art. The Young American Awards are given each year to young adults between the ages of fifteen and twenty-two who have achieved exceptional excellence in the fields of science, religion, service, government, business, athletics, art, music or literature. Miss Stroud, a twenty-year-old member of the Western Cherokee tribe in Oklahoma, was one of six to receive the award.

June 6. A handful of Indians were arrested shortly after about forty Indians had set up camp on the top of Mt. Rushmore National Memorial. The arrested individuals demanded that the government honor an 1868 Sioux treaty that declared all land in South Dakota west of the Missouri River belonged to the Indians. The Indians were charged with climbing the monument -- a misdemeanor.

June 11. Thirty-five U.S. marshalls removed fifteen Indians from Alcatraz Island, located in the waters off San Francisco, thereby ending a nineteen-month occupation of the former federal prison. The basis for this action on the part of the native Americans was their contention that a treaty privilege gave them unused government lands. The Indian group had been hoping to get use of the land after negotiations with federal officials and use the place for an Indian cultural center.

In late June the Commissioner of Indian Affairs announced the appointment of John Artichocker, a Sioux, as area director of the Bureau's office in Phoenix. He was the holder of BS and MA degrees from the University of South Dakota, and was a career employee of the BIA. In 1964 he won one of the U.S. Junior Chamber of Commerce's prestigious "Ten Outstanding Men of the Year Awards."

In the summer, Columbia University in New York City sponsored its fourth Summer Program in Broadcast Journalism for Members of Minority Groups. For the first time American Indians were among the participants. The program guaranteed full time TV or radio employment in stations across the country for graduates of the eleven week session who went to Columbia's Graduate School of Journalism for training in all aspects of broadcast news. The program provided free tuition and room and board on the Columbia campus. The program had no formal educational requirements and participants did not necessarily have to have college degrees. The first three Indians who participated were Lorraine Edmo, Shoshone-Bannock, who was to be employed at KID-TV in Idaho Falls; Tanna Beebe, Cowlitz, who would go to KIRO-TV in Seattle; and Donald Savage, Chippewa, who was a news cameraman at WDSM-TV in Duluth and who planned to return there later in September as a newsman.

July 1. Approximately one hundred Indians who had taken over several buildings at a one-time Nike missle site near Chicago on June 14, were removed by 150 armed policemen. The occupation took place as a protest against the lack of housing available in the area. A few days later, on July 30, a somewhat smaller group of Indians, alleged to have been the same group, peacefully took over another abandoned Nike site in nearby Hinsdale.

July 12. Dr. James J. Wilson III assumed his new duties as executive director of the Southwestern Cooperative Educational Laboratory, after having served for the prior six years as director of the Indian Division of the Office of Economic Opportunity. Dr. Wilson was a former professor of education at Chadron State College, Nebraska, and had served in the navy. Married, the father of six children, he was named "Outstanding Young Indian Man," in 1969 by the National Congress of American Indians.

July 16. Commissioner of Indian Affairs Louis R. Bruce announced that since July 1970, American Indians had started 241 new businesses and expanded 143 Indian owned businesses through the Indian Business Development Fund program of the Bureau of Indian Affairs. He estimated that the new developments would create almost 3,000 Indian jobs, with an annual payroll of about 12 million dollars. The purpose of the Fund was to provide initial capital, on a grant basis, to Indians for establishing new permanent businesses or for expanding existing enterprises on or near reservations. Only profit making enterprises were eligible.

July 23. Secretary of the Interior Rogers C.B. Morton announced the appointment of John O. Crow as Commissioner of the Bureau of Indian Affairs. Fifty-nine years old, Crow was one-fourth Cherokee and grew up in Commerce, Oklahoma. He was a graduate of Haskell Institute and later played professional football with the Boston Redskins, now the Washington Redskins. Crow was to be responsible for running the internal operation of the Bureau. He had previously served in many other BIA positions with various assignments, while having earned several prestigious government awards.

July 30. Interior Secretary Rogers C.B. Morton and HUD Secretary George Romney signed an agreement reaffirming a government committment to improve housing conditions for Indians, by clearing the way for the expenditure of 40,000 dollars for the preparation of a laymen and professionals' manual which would cover all relevant programs, indicating their nature, statutory basis, qualifications for assistance, and Federal officials at the national, state or local levels administering each program. The two agencies jointly operate a five year plan to provide 6,000 dwellings a year for the Indians. Secretary Morton pointed out, "that about 45,000 Indian families live in dwellings that do not meet either health or safety standards. One cannot emerge from the destructive force of poverty without decent housing." He concluded the remarks by saying, "Interior is committed to reassuring Indians that by the end of this decade all Indian reservation families will have proper housing."

The newest and most advanced polytechnic institute in the United States, Southwestern Indian Polytechnical Institute (SIPI), was opened on August 21 at Albuquerque, New Mexico, with the dedication of the BIA's new $14 million, 164 acre facility, located on the outskirts of the city. Assistant Secretary of the Interior Harrison Loesch commended the planners, "A great number of people have worked together, shared ideas and given their time and talents, laboring for us to this day. The contribution of Indian people to the development of this school is especially pleasing. They have been substantially involved in every stage of its planning and growth. The original idea came from Indian leaders." The Institute was planned to offer unique post-secondary training to members of more than sixty Indian tribes when classes began on September 16. An enrollment of 700 students was expected. Courses in the school were employment oriented and directed towards jobs that exist and the kinds of skills that are required for those jobs. Programs for each student were to be individually structured to meet his personal education needs and to enable him to reach his educational goal as quickly as possible. John L. Peterson, former director of vocational-technical education programs at the Phoenix Indian High School, became the first superintendent.

Late August found Indian groups angry, frustrated, and in despair at the BIA's decision to transfer Indian water specialist William Veeder to Phoenix, Arizona, despite the protests of every major Indian group and leader in the country. Observers noted that Indian influence was "zero" when the reclamationists, water hungry municipalities, the livestock industry and men who represent them in Congress got upset over the outspoken and controversial Veeder's contention that Indians "are being planned out of existence" in the West. The center of the dispute concerns the role Veeder was playing in behalf of several main stream pueblos excluded from a multiple suit brought to set a precedent on Indian water rights on the tributaries of the Rio Grande. Veeder has also warned that the Washoe Project will dry up Pyramid Lake -- a controversy that the department had been studying for years without a decision.

A National Indian Training Center was opened on September 1, located on the campus of Intermountain School, a BIA facility located at Brigham Center, Utah. The center was expected to enroll upwards of 500 Indians annually for in-service and preparatory training for Indian men and women seeking employment and advancement in federal, state, and tribal government jobs. The Bureau of Indian Affairs and the U.S. Civil Service Commission would jointly operate the Center.

In September the School of Public Health, University of California at Berkeley, commenced the offering of ten traineeships to American Indians for the graduate degree of Master of Public Health. The University felt that, with the growing need for improved health service for all Americans, there was an increased need for trained professionals drawn from all quarters. It was deemed important that this training be made available to American Indians who were interested in working among Indian people in responsible planning, or administrative positions.

Pledging to institute a series of reforms, Interior Secretary Rogers Morton on October 4 said that he would implement programs designed to overcome Indian criticism of the BIA. He asked for a new Indian water rights office, with an initial year's operating budget of $2 million, to protect reservations from competing federal and commercial water interests. He visualized the new office as preparing the paper work for suits to be prosecuted by the Justice Department. He further avowed to vigorously fight for BIA budget requests for an expanded road building plan to assist those economically isolated Indian communities without present convenient and normal access to the outside world. Morton in his announcement stated his intentions of creating a fifteen man advisory board, which would include representatives of national Indian organizations, to insure improved communications between the BIA, his own office and the community.

October 9. The prestigious Ford Foundation reported that it was funding a six-year, $100 million program to aid minority education. The grant would involve about eighty per cent of the foundation's spending for general higher education in 1973-78. About forty million dollars of the grant would be used to support scholarships and fellowships for blacks, Puerto Ricans, Mexican-Americans and American Indians at the upperclass and graduate level.

December 16. An unprecedented union of Native Americans, the Coalition of Organized Indians and Natives (COINS) was formed in Washington, D.C., to set strategy for Indians in the crucial 1970s. The new organization planned to establish a common front on issues facing the Native Americans and to create a common political strategy for the 1972 election year. Included in COINS were the National Congress of American Indians (NCAI), the American Indian Movement (AIM), and the National Indian Youth Council (NIYC), together with many other Indian organizations.

In a history-making act, President Nixon signed into law on December 18 an Alaska native land settlement bill, following the approval vote of the Federation of Alaska Natives. Congress had passed the measure a few days earlier. The signing of the bill into law meant that a freeze on Alaska state land acquisition of the previous administration had been lifted. The bill provided for a total of 962.5 million dollars ($462.5 million of that amount over the forthcoming eleven years from the federal government and the remainder from state mineral revenues at the rate of two percent a year). Forty million acres of land and mineral rights were to be selected by the natives, most of which would be close to their villages. The money and land were to be governed by twelve regional native corporations. The Secretary of the Interior was given power to assign eighty million acres for potential recreation and conservation use, subject to Congressional approval within five years, and to set aside an 800 mile corridor should he accept and agree to a proposed oil pipeline. Opposition to the bill included the Arctic Slope Native Association, composed of 4500 Eskimos from the North Slope area who were allowed only surface rights to their oil-rich lands, with compensating subsurface rights elsewhere. (The association had instituted suit on October 5 claiming full rights to the oil-bearing land on the North Slope.)

1972

Early in the year the Mohawk Nation (NY) held trials to rule-off the reservation young traditionals at Akwesasne and another to remove Rarihokwats (a newspaper editor) from their land. (He later won his case.)

In January, the Dartmouth College Alumni Council, the fifty-three member "Senate" representing the college's 36,000 living alumni, heard eloquent testimony by native American Dartmouth students that continued use of the Indian symbol (at the college) represented an offensive distortion of their culture and history. Recognizing the student's concern and also that most alumni regard the symbol as a positive depiction honoring both the Indian and Dartmouth's early history, the council voted to establish an "ad hoc" committee to consider the matter. (Many positive changes occured without demands or confrontations.)

In January, Charles Trimble executive director of the NCAI told 300 Indian leaders at Denver's Cosmopolitan Hotel that the redesign of the BIA had been carved out in a "clandestine manner." He claimed that no Indian organization had been involved in the actions and despite offers of cooperation, they had been ignored.

January 11. The Rev. Harold Stephen Jones, a Sioux, was consecrated as suffragan bishop of the Episcopal Diocese of South Dakota. One thousand persons attended the ceremony where the South Dakota born clergyman became the first American Indian elevated to the office of bishop.

Clark Gruening, attorney for the Chugach Native Association (Alaska) people disputed Rogers C.B. Morton's claim that the withdrawal of 80 million acres from use was the "right way to go for the Native people." Gruening felt that seventy percent of the land reserved by the Interior Department was made up of glaciers and mountain tops, rather than "lands similar in character to those on which a village is located," as required by the Lands Claims Act.

June 7. Dean Edward Wade, Flandreau-Santee Sioux, was graduated from the U.S. Military Academy at West Point, New York. He was one of four cadets enrolled with Indian lineage.

Navajo self-rule was offered on July 17 by Anthony Lincoln, director of Navajo affairs in the Bureau of Indian Affairs. He proffered an opportunity to the Indians to give to the Navajos control of all BIA operations in their area. Included was a 110 million dollar annual budget. The bid was seen as a victory for the self-determination forces which operate within the bureau headed by Louis Bruce, the commissioner. To that date, only two tribes had previously acquired complete control of all programs affecting their reservation -- the Miccosukee (FL) and the Zuni (NM). Neither compared in size with the 25,000 square mile Navajo reservation which covers parts of the states of Arizona, New Mexico and Utah, and has a population of 134,000.

In August, a calm AIM national meeting held in White Oak (OK) ended without problems which had been feared. Elected as national AIM Chairman was Carter Camp, twenty-nine years old. He replaced Vern Bellecourt who remained on the important policy-making board of directors. John Trudell was elected co-chairman.

November 2. A group of approximately 500 Indians, mostly young people, arrived in Washington after a trek across the country. . . "A Trail of Broken Treaties". . . for a planned week of demonstrations hoping to promote public demands for reform in the BIA and get Congressional action on a program of twenty demands, which included treaty adjustments, land policy changes and social and economic programs. The protestors were headed by activists in the American Indian Movement, who are supposed to be mostly urban Indians. The leaders of the Indians used the first day to negotiate with federal officials for temporary lodgings, food and money, and for plans to hold memorial services for Indians buried at the Arlington National Cemetary. (The U.S. Court of Appeals ruled three days later in favor of the Indians' petition for the use of the cemetary for memorial services.) A tentative agreement to use certain federal buildings collapsed after scuffles took place between demonstrators and capitol police who attempted to lock the doors of the BIA building. The Indians successfully evaded the guardians of the building and locked themselves inside. They refused a district court order to leave. On November 6, U.S. District Court Judge John H. Pratt judged the Indians to be guilty of contempt of court. The contempt action was held in abeyance by the action of the U.S. Court of Appeals until November 8, by which time White House action and public attention created a climate for an agreement to leave the BIA premises. The federal officials claimed that over two million dollars in damages were caused to their building. Thousands of pounds of documents had been removed and about 700,000 dollars worth of art and artifacts had been removed during the occupation period. (Much of the removed items gradually wound up in the hands of the government in a number of ways and places across the country.)

Late in the year Indians were encouraged to take money while the taking was still good (bonuses, rentals with a floor of one dollar per acre and royalties of 17.5 cents a ton). The Northern Cheyenne Tribe let out a contract to the Peabody, Amax, Consol, Norsworthy & Regner and Bruce Ennis; a total of 243,808 acres of coal -- a startling fifty-six percent of the reservation's entire acreage. The tribal officials are alleged to have been influenced by BIA officials who said "there are indications coal will be a saleable product for only a few years."

In a December 2 public reaction to the occupation of the BIA offices in Washington and other factors, Interior Secretary Rogers Morton took away "all present authority for Indian Affairs from Commissioner Louis Bruce, Assistant Secretary Harrison A. Loesch and Deputy BIA Commissioner John O. Crow. (Crow had earlier, on November 30, called Bruce incompetant, while both he and Loesch had publicly decried Bruce's action during the Washington fracas. Bruce had indeed expressed support for some of the militant's aims. The Morton action was seen as an attempt to placate the militant Indian groups who had cried out for the Crow and Loesch removal, citing their opposition to moves to get more Indian control over BIA programs.) All three submitted official resignations which were announced to the press on December 8.

1973   Early in the new year the American Indian Movement (AIM) which had previously centered its activities in urban areas, focused attention on Oklahoma and plains state reservations.

January 9. The administration officially refused to accept the twenty demands submitted by the Trail of Broken Promises, a group composed of about 1,000 "militant" Indians who had occupied the Bureau of Indian Affairs Headquarters in Washington for seven days in November, 1972. In a letter delivered to Hank Adams, Indian leader, the Nixon administration stated that the demands had been found either unacceptable or had already been acted upon. The letter concluded with the statement that Indians had lost any rights to negotiate or renegotiate treaties, as demanded by the group, because these had been granted citizenship in 1924 and reforms had already started.

January 24. The Ninth U.S. Court of Appeals reversed a lower court decision regarding three Indians accused of selling copper wire during the occupation of Alcatraz Island in November, 1969.

In February, FBI Agents in the Nation's capitol arrested Hank Adams, an Indian Activist, and Les Whitten, a reporter, as they loaded boxes of government papers into Whitten's car preparatory to returning them to the BIA. The records had been taken by Indians in the Trail of Broken Treaties sit-in demonstration of the BIA headquarters in November, 1972. Adams was not an original protestor at the November break-in, and went to Washington to gain data and finish a book in preparation. As tempers were fanned to fever pitch between government officers and Indians, Adams offered to be a intermediary and hopefully avoid bloodshed and violence. For over a month Adams reportedly worked to get the return of the government materials, after all Indians had safely returned to their homes. He appeared to be the only Indian person sensitive to the need to return the stolen documents, but found himself charged with possession of stolen papers by the FBI agents.

February 6. The Custer County (SD) Courthouse was damaged by fire and the Chamber of Commerce building was burned down. Trouble began when police blocked a group of native American people from entering the court building for a conference with the District Attorney about charges against a white man accused in the knife slaying of an Oglala, Wesley Bad Heart Bull. Russell Means was arrested on charges of assault with a dangerous weapon, conspiracy, and participating in a riot. Vern Bellecourt was charged with conspiracy. Dennis Banks was also named in a sealed indictment. The Grand Jury dismissed riot and arson charges against twenty-two other persons for lack of evidence. The man charged with slaying Bull was eventually found innocent of second degree manslaughter, but Bull's mother found a more serious charge filed against her for protesting her son's murder!

February 27. Members of the American Indian Movement (AIM) and some activist supporters seized and occupied the tiny place of Wounded Knee, located on the Oglala Sioux Reservation in South Dakota, and remained there until May 8. (The site was the place where about 300 Indians, including women and children, were killed by a U.S. cavalry unit.) During this period of intense confrontation between AIM proponents and federal officials, two Indians were killed, ten wounded, two federal marshalls were wounded, about 300

Indians were arrested, and a reported $240,000 in damages to Indian homes.

February 27 -- Wounded Knee . . . insurgents demanded that the U.S. Senate Foreign Relations Committee hold hearings on treaties made with the Indians and that the Senate hold a full scale investigation of government treatment of Indians. After many failures, an agreement was signed on May 5, calling for the removal of government weapons carriers and a surrender of all weapons by the Indians. The town was completely evacuated on May 8.

In March, former presidential candidate George McGovern, faced with a serious problem in his attempt to gain reelection to the U.S. Senate, spoke to white voters in Huron, South Dakota, and called for strong actions against what he called AIM's "violent lawbreakers."

In mid-March, the Wounded Knee Legal Defense-Offense Committee, composed of about twenty-five lawyers, researchers and secretarial assistants, was founded to protect and defend 445 persons arrested in the occupation or activity related to Wounded Knee -- as well as to commence a legal offensive designed to change long, defective Oglala Sioux-U.S. relationships. Included in the group were attorneys Ramon Roubideaux, Rapid City; Ken Tilsen; St. Paul; Beverly Axelrod, San Francisco; and Mark Lane, New York attorney and author of <u>Rush to Judgement</u>.

On Sunday, March 26, about half of the 4,000 worshippers were Indians attending a "Native American Mass," at New York's Cathedral Church of St. John the Devine. Seven Sioux chiefs there to plead the case of the Wounded Knee protestors at the United Nations were included and housed there by the church officers. "May your cause be heard by all the people in America," said the Dean of the Cathedral.

During the forty-fifth annual motion pictures awards of the Academy of Motion Picture Arts and Sciences in Los Angeles on March 27, actor Marlon Brando created a stir when he refused the best actor award. Sacheen Littlefeather read a statement by Brando in which he protested the media's and the nation's treatment of American Indians.

The right to tax Indian incomes was limited by a March 27 Supreme Court ruling which unanimously stated that the state of Arizona could not apply a state income tax on Indians who earned their total livelihood on their reservations. (The state had alleged that one member of the Navajo nation owed it $16.20 in state income taxes for the year 1967.) In its epoch decision, the U.S. high court ruled that laws and treaties had to be read against a backdrop of tribal sovereignty and in a judicial tradition of resolving doubts, "in favor of the weak and defenseless people who are wards of the nation." In a separate ruling on the same date, the federal court said that the gross receipts from Indian-owned enterprises off reservations were taxable by states. (This ruling resulted from a case concerning a Mescalero Apache owned ski resort adjacent to the Mescalero Apache reservation in New Mexico.)

In April, the first stage of a BIA reorganization authorized immediate staffing of certain positions in order to implement the president's directive to reduce non-essential Central Office support staff, and increase day-to-day operational activities of the bureau from Washington to the field offices. Included in the new revamping were six major offices: Indian Education Programs, Tribal Resource Development, Trust Responsibilities, Indian Services, Public Affairs and Administration.

An apparent truce in the Wounded Knee incident which appeared to be headed for an end and a setting-up of preliminary talks in Washington was disrupted on April 17, when three unidentified airplanes dropped supplies to the occupying Indians. Shooting again broke out between the disputants.

In May the Thunderbird American Indian Dancers were requested by the state of New York to make suggestions as to how the state could perform more effectively in serving urban Indians and their city organizations. Among the suggestions sent to Albany was an Indian desk in the state government, staffed by Indians to administer the program. It was revealed that though the private sector has a minimal program, the state affords urban Indians no help.

A report issued on June 24 by the Federal Trade Commission (FTC) charged that unfair trade and credit practices by operators of reservation trading posts had severely worsened the long-time poverty of the Navajo Indians. The report zeroed in on the failure of the BIA to enforce consumer protection regulations and advocated that primary enforcement be turned over to the Navajo tribe. (Historically most of the businesses mentioned in the report did their business through a permit system of the BIA.) The FTC announcement pointed out that trading post prices exceeded the national average by twenty-seven percent and the nearest off-reservation stores by 16.6 percent. The report also claimed that an "unscrupulous minority" of traders had engaged in questionable credit practices such as inducing Indians to have welfare and Social Security checks sent directly to their post to cover credit purchases.

July 17. The U.S Census Bureau released a report which revealed that an analysis of the 1970 data showed that Indians continued to bring up the rear in most economic and social areas in spite of significant advances in education since the 1960 census figures were reported. Their data showed the 1969 median income for Indian families was $5,832.00, which compared to the national median of $9,590.00; forty percent of all Indian families were living below the poverty level, as compared to fourteen percent of all families and about thirty-two percent of black families; ninety-five percent of Indian children aged seven to thirteen years and more than half the Indians aged three to thirty-four years were attending schools in 1970, with the number attending college doubling since 1960.

July 20. Vern Bellecourt was arrested in Chicago's O'Hare International Airport on his return from Europe and enroute to the national AIM meeting in White Oak, Oklahoma. He was charged in connection with speeches he made at Colorado State University in Fort Collins, urging students to take food and medical supplies to Wounded Knee.

July 26. In Philadelphia four Iroquois iron workers were acquitted of charges of assaulting police after the jury viewed film of the incident which had been made by a

Hollywood movie crew. One additional iron worker, Leroy Shenadoah, twenty-four, an Onondaga, was shot and killed during the assault. His death was later ruled "justifiable." The Iroquois group had gathered on a balcony of the hotel where they stayed to watch a movie being made in the street below. From somewhere in the hotel a mattress was thrown down, and police went to the balcony to remove the Indians. In court the police stated that the Iroquois resisted arrest and force was required to subdue them. Shenadoah was killed in the struggle. After three weeks of testimony, the jury took only two hours to acquit Raymond Moses, twenty, Maynard Gabriel, twenty-six, Morris Crouse, twenty-five, and John Benedict, twenty-six. Benedict was from Akwesasne and the others were Onondagas. After police testimony was completed, the defense announced a previously unknown fact, the movie crew had swung around and the entire incident was on film. It completely discredited the testimony of the police.

July 30. Dennis Banks, speaking to members of the AIM at Tulsa airport, said his organization would move in a massive effort to influence legislation which would seek to repeal the 1934 Indian Reorganization Act and the abolishment of the BIA. By July 4, 1976, the AIM would call for the cancellation of key contracts and leases on reservations, free elections for all tribal positions, boycotts of non-Indian businesses and closing of BIA operated schools. Alternative schools would be established. The non-Indian businesses would be "nationalized."

In August the Northern Cheyenne Indians wondered if the energy crisis of Euro/American people would spell out their doom. Under the tan sandstone buttes and the rolling, grassy river bottoms of the 415,000 acre reservation — an isolated 100 miles east of Billings, Montana, which they struggled for until it was finally awarded to them in 1884 -- lies a large deposit of coal. The coal is important because it is low in sulphur and can be burned to generate electricity without violating federal air pollution levels in sulphur emissions. Some experts believe that the enormous Fort Union basin of Montana, Wyoming, and the Dakotas is one of the few places in the United States where one can still get some sense of how it was before the white man came, and it could become the largest industrial development in the world. James E. Parker, Bureau of Reclamation, said the power developments alone might be the largest in the world. It would produce one-seventh of the electricity now used in the United States. Tom Gardner, thirty-seven-year-old Cheyenne anti-poverty and community action director saw, "prosperity from the coal, but the white man's extinction of our way of life."

August 5. Governor Richard Kneep of South Dakota, bending to public pressure, announced that the sacred religious Sun Dance Ceremony had been cancelled at the long publicized announced site on an 800 acre parcel of private land adjoining the Crazy Horse Mountain. This forced a move to the Rosebud Reservation, where a peaceful four days of ceremonies and discussions were held. Non-native people were turned away with few exceptions. Filming, taping, photography, alcohol, drugs, and fire arms were successfully kept out, due to a tight, vigilant Indian security move.

The creation of an Office of Indian Rights was announced by the U.S. Department of Justice on August 13, with the department's civil rights division being the supervising force for the new thrust. The plan envisioned that the new office would serve as a coordinator for most Indian affairs previously handled by other offices in the department and would start legislation required. Carl Stoiber, a civil rights division attorney, was appointed to head the new office, with R. Dennis Ickes being named as the deputy director. (Acknowledging that neither of the new division chiefs were Indian, Assistant Attorney General J. Stanley Pottinger said an effort would be made to recruit some.)

August 15. Gerald Millard, twenty, and Alan Duran, eighteen, were beaten in an incident in Custer, South Dakota, by former Deputy Sheriff Clayton Mostiller in broad daylight. Mostiller attacked the pair with a bull whip for no apparent reason and after a savage beating, whipped Millard around the neck and dragged him forty feet with his horse. The action was allegedly witnessed by Mostiller's employer,

Ray Miller, of T & R Rides. Stunned, shocked and beaten, the two young men walked into town for assistance and were promptly arrested for public intoxication and held without bond. When notified of the incident, attorneys Mark Lane and Russel Means went to Custer to talk to local officials. After three hours of argument, state's attorney Hobart Gates reluctantly agreed to file formal felony complaints against the former lawman and his employer. But there was to be no trial for the white men, for when the Custer Grand Jury met it declined to indict them and all charges were dismissed.

In late August primary elections held on the Rosebud Reservation, South Dakota, saw Bob Burnette, who had often supported the activities of the AIM, topping Webster Two Hawk, a vocal anti-AIM, for the presidency. Final elections were to be held in October. The tribe also voted in favor of permitting eighteen year olds to vote in tribal elections.

The AIM gained and lost strength as the result of a series of unrelated hearings and tragic events. First, the allegations of many of the movement's critics that the organization was dead were proven wrong. Second, Clyde Bellecourt, thirty-six, an Anishawbe from Minneapolis, was shot and critically wounded on August 27 on the Rosebud (Sioux) reservation, South Dakota.

On August 27, at Winner, South Dakota, -- population estimated to be about 3700 White residents and 350 natives -- the Ministerial Alliance and the Chamber of Commerce joined together and refused a request for food to feed a group of about eighty persons who had come there to protect Clyde Bellecourt from possible further harm. The hospital -- a Baptist institution -- demanded that Bellecourt be removed, even though his physician said that to do so would jeopardize his life. The hospital administrators rescinded their action when the attending doctors said they would resign from the staff if the officials persisted in such rank action.

The Oklahoma Human Rights Commission on September 6 urged that state schools abolish rules forcing native students to cut their hair because codes "promote racial friction and community divisiveness." The OHRC said that it had received about thirty inquiries on the matter totally from Indian students. "The school boards," it said, "haven't asked for any advice whatsoever."

September 29. The U.S. House Interior Committee approved a bill to restore Federal services to the Menominees who had lost their status under a 1961 Act of Congress during a termination-minded administration. Vine Deloria, Jr., well known native author, talked enthusiastically about the need to recognize once more, at a meeting of DRUMS (Determination of Rights and Unity of Menominee Stockholders).

December 3. Morris Thompson, thirty-four, an Athabascan Indian, was appointed Commissioner of Indian Affairs. Born in Tanawa, Alaska, he attended the University of Alaska where he majored in Civil Engineering and minored in political science.

December 3. The new BIA Commissioner appointed the first Indian woman Superintendent as his first official act of office. Mrs. Shirley Plume, an Oglala Sioux, was named to head the Standing Rock (ND) Agency.

December 28. President Richard Nixon signed a comprehensive manpower training and jobs act which had passed Congress December 20. One important provision of the bill was its authorization of special assistance for certain hard-hit segments of the labor market, including Indians.

1974   An analysis of the 1970 U.S. Census Report revealed a shocking tale of continued neglect and unconcern about the condition of the Indian minorities in this country. Some highlights included were:

a) Fifty thousand Indian families live in unsanitary dilapidated dwellings; many in huts, shanties, even abandoned automobiles.

b) The unemployment rate among Indians was nearly 40 percent -- more than ten times the national average.

c) The average life expectancy of an American Indian was 64 years; for all other Americans it was 70.5.

d) Forty-two percent of Indian school children -- almost double the national average -- drop out before completing high school.

e) The problems of Indian education are many: Ten percent of American Indians over age 14 have had no education at all. Nearly 60 percent have less than an eighth grade education.

f) The infant mortality rate is 30.9 for 1,000 live births for Indians and Alaskan natives as contrasted with 21.9 for all other races in America.

g) Fifty percent of Indian families have cash incomes below $2,000 a year, 75 percent below $3,000.

h) The incidence of new active cases of tuberculosis among Indians and Alaskan natives outpaces the national average by seven times. Twenty-nine percent of Indian homes rely upon unsatisfactory sources of water and more than 50 percent of all Indian homes have inadequate sanitary waste disposal facilities.

In January, following public hearings at Denver, Colorado, in December, 1973, BIA Commissioner Thompson instituted a streamlined system for the use or distribution of judgements to American Indian tribes or groups, by the Indian Claims Commission or the U.S. Court of Claims.

January 19. BIA Commissioner Morris Thompson said, "restoration of federal services to the Menominee tribe is now official, and it is a landmark decision for the Congress. I would like you to know that this is the first time in history that a decision of this kind has been made; to restore services after a period of termination."

February. At a press conference on the 1975 F.Y. Indian budget, the Under Secretary of Interior, John C. Whitaker said, "since 1969, Federal outlays in Indian programs have soared from approximately .8 billion dollars annually to some $1.6 billion requested for fiscal year 1975."

March. Vine Deloria, Jr., noted Indian author, wrote that "in one gigantic leap (S.J.Res.133) put Congress in the forefront of the Indian movement by proposing a vehicle more daring and creative regarding the American Indian Policy Review Commission, than even the Indians had conceived."

Speaking to the Northwest Affiliated Tribal Councils in March, BIA Commissioner Thompson guaranteed trust relationship. "Many people are concerned that by assuming the control and responsibility to operate more and more of their own programs they may jeopardize their trust relationship with the federal government. My feeling is just the opposite situation will take place. Indians now have the opportunity to place a higher priority on the trust protection services they wish to provide by identifying this priority in their budget priorities and narratives and their operational plans."

April. President Nixon signed the Indian Financing Act of 1974. The law consolidated existing revolving loan funds already administered by the Bureau of Indian Affairs and authorized the appropriation of an additional $50 million.

April 8. A legal opinion issued by Interior Department Acting Solicitor David E. Lindgren denied that the Southwestern Indian Polytechnic Institute (SIPI) was required to admit non-Indian students from New Mexico's tri-cultural population. (A short-lived activist occupation earlier had made such claim as part of its grievances.)

May. Mohawks seized a 612 acre site in the Adirondack State Park (Big Moose, N.Y.) using an old girl's camp buildings for shelter. White reaction caused an exchange of claims and counter-claims, and some incidents.

May. Clarence Antioquia, thirty-four, a Tlingit Indian, was named Director of the Juneau Alaska Area Office of the Bureau of Indian Affairs.

June. Jose A. Zuni, Isleta Pueblo Indian, was named Director of Administration of the Bureau of Indian Affairs.

June. The BIA published A History of Indian Policy, by Dr. S. Lyman Tyler, head of the American West Center, University of Utah.

July. Francis E. Briscoe, fifty-six, a member of the Caddo Tribe, was named BIA Area Director of the Portland Area Office.

August. A decision was announced which ended a long dispute and gave the Chemehuevi tribe equitable title to eighteen miles of shoreline along Lake Havasu, a portion of the Colorado River, about forty miles northeast of Needles (CA).

Bilingual education for Indians was stimulated in August, through passage of amendments to the Elementary and Secondary Education Act of 1965. The new amendments would provide for the programs in Indian schools operated by the BIA and those operated by tribes themselves.

September. The BIA Commissioner pointed out that the new part of the Code of Federal Regulations, "is like our Constitutional Bill of Rights for the BIA students."

September 16. Charges against AIM Wounded Knee defendants Dennis Banks and Russell C. Means were dismissed by U.S. Judge Fred J. Nichols. The judge said that during the trial the FBI had been shown to lie and suborn perjury.

September 19. At midnight, the sixty-seven member Bonners Ferry Kootenais (Idaho) band of Indians declared war against the U.S. government, and demanded a 128,000 acre reservation, a treaty, payment for 1.6 million acres of lost aboriginal lands and recognition of hunting, fishing, water and other aboriginal rights. They had to set up pickets along the highways to collect ten cent tolls from motorists passing through their territory. They emphasized that theirs was a war against the government and not against the "suyapi," the white people.

October. Thomas J. Ellison, fifty, Oklahoma Choctaw, was named area director of the BIA's Muskogee, Oklahoma, Area Office.

In an October ceremony, the Crow Indian Tribe of Montana honored Secretary of the Interior Rogers C.B. Morton, as an "Advocate of the American Indian," for his leadership in promoting Indian self-determination and his role in the Alaska Native Claims Settlement.

November. BIA Commissioner Thompson said, "A cooperative effort by the Bureau, Indian tribes, and professional consultants have developed a three-stage format for inventorying water resources affecting reservations. Title to 3,500 acres of Fort Mojave Reservation land is being returned to the tribe following the acknowledgement that the land was taken 50 years ago as a result of a faulty land survey." The hunting, fishing and boating rights of the Colville and Spokane Tribes in Lake Roosevelt were also restored.

December. Harley M. Frankel, thirty-three, was appointed new deputy commissioner of the Bureau of Indian Affairs. His duties were to primarily be management and administration of the widely diverse functions of the bureau.

BIA Commissioner Thompson, in a Christmas press release, noted that there were "16,000 Indians now in college with higher education assistance from the Bureau."

1975   January. Years after the initial issuance of permits to five coal companies to have access to Crow Reservation tribally owned coal underneath about ten percent of their land, the BIA provided the first environmental impact statement. It said that, "adverse impacts would be (a) dilution of the Crow's way of life through increased industrial activity." It further reported, "this could mean the loss of cultural heritage and even eventual extinction of the Crow language." (The tribe later filed suit asking the BIA commissioner and the BIA to cancel the leases and permits already granted.)

January 1. Members of the Menominee Warriors Society occupied the Alexian Brothers Novitiate, Grisham, Wisconsin. They ended the matter and left on February 3, after the novitiate had agreed to deed them the place feeling that they had brought public notice to their cause. Circuit Court Judge

Gordon Myse stated that he went to the building and told the Indians he had authorized a telephone tap so their calls would be intercepted. "This was done," he said, "to prevent them from saying things they shouldn't have over the line. It was not for evidentiary purposes." (On July 9, the Alexians cancelled the deal.)

January 4. President Ford signed into law the Indian Self-Determination and Education Assistance Act (P.L.93-638). The act was considered by many to be the most important legislation for Native Americans since passage of the Indian Reorganization Act of 1934. Title II of the Act gives the Indian communities a stronger role in approving or disapproving the use of Special Assistance Funds for Indian children in public schools.

January 6. The last full-blooded member of the Mandan Tribe, Mrs. Mattie Grinnell, who lived to the age of 108 years old, died in Twin Buttes, North Dakota. She was born at Like-A-Fish-Hook village on the Fort Berthold Reservation one year after the Civil War. The BIA felt that she was virtually certain to have been the last person to have received approval for a Civil War Widow's pension. Interesting to note was that Mrs. Grinnell in 1968 at the age of 101 took part in the Poor People's March on Washington.

In late February, AIM activists occupied the Fairchild Semi-Conductor Plant at Shiprock, New Mexico, for several days and left March 3, on the promise that they would not be prosecuted. Claims as to the damages sustained to the plant and use of the telephones were widely ranged. The AIM members had entered the plant to demand that 140 Navajos who had been laid off be rehired, but their efforts only resulted in the firm ultimately closing down operations, leaving all Indians without work and with bitter feelings.

March 6. Environmental Protection Agency Administrator Russell S. Train signed a memorandum which provided a way for Indian tribes and organizations to carry their environmental concerns directly to his agency.

Indian leaders throughout the country met in March, April, and May in Washington, D.C., with representatives of the

BIA and the Indian Health Service to plan implementation of the Indian Self-Determination and Education Assistance Act (P.L.93-638). The act gives tribes the right to plan and operate Indian programs for themselves under contract with the federal government.

Nearly 200 Tribal representatives met in Washington April 2-4, for the National Conference on Indian Water Rights, jointly sponsored by the National Tribal Chairmen's Association (NTCA) and the National Congress of American Indians (NCAI). The Conference showed a unity of purpose rarely witnessed in Indian national politics. The Conference made available a forum for the documentation and itemization of specific water rights in Indian country and provided a public platform for dialogue, often confrontational in nature between tribal and governmental officials.

April 2. The Omaha tribe reclaimed 3190 acres of rich crop land by moving houses into the area, preparatory to planting of the land, and commenced drawing up land leases despite challenges in Iowa State Court by non-Indians who also claimed title. The Omaha's rights to the land was upheld in an unsigned nine page Interior Department Solicitor's Report which concluded that the non-Indians who resided on the "Blackbird Bend" (called by the Indians "Old People's Land") "have no rights now."

April 21. The Burnham Chapter members of the Navajo Nation again voted their opposition, for the third time in two years, to the proposals of two major gasification companies to build eight plants and related commercial outlets in the Burnham, New Mexico, area.

April 29. The Quechan Indian Nation's Tribal president, Elmer M. Savilla, said, "we will no longer tolerate the injustices perpetrated by the United States against us. The Quechans no longer will be the peaceful little tribe along the Colorado River." The Colorado River's mid-point marks the eastern boundary of the Fort Yuma Reservation in California, homeland of about 1,000 Quechans. They were seeking to establish their ownership of about 500 acres of contested land in a suit brought by the tribe against

California's Imperial County and the Imperial Irrigation District in U.S. Court. The issue was only a part of a larger and long-standing dispute in the Department of Interior and with the California governmental bodies.

May 22. The Bureau of Indian Affairs bowed to months of pressure and announced a decision to keep open for an additional year the Intermountain Boarding School at Brigham City, Utah.

June. The All-Indian Pueblo Council told Indian Commissioner Morris Thompson that unless he appointed a director for the important Albuquerque, New Mexico, Area Office by June 30, it would sue for damages claiming breach of trust responsibility by the BIA to the twenty-four tribes within that jurisdiction.

June 23 and 24. Tribal witnesses gave their views and answered questions before the Senate Sub-Committee on Indian Affairs holding hearings on S.B.1328 and attempted to answer the question: "Should Indian Tribes seek to reacquire jurisdiction over all persons within their reservation boundaries from the states which have held that jurisdiction since 1953 under the Termination-oriented Public Law 280?"

In July about 300 Indians spontaneously decided to occupy the Interior Department Building in Portland, Oregon, during a march seeking to protest the "campaign of war and aggression against Indian people being waged by the U.S. government against Indians of the Rosebud and Pine Ridge, South Dakota, reservations. (They only stayed twenty-four hours and left peacefully feeling that they had gotten public notice and thus accomplished their mission.)

July 14. The Federal Communications Commission (FCC) granted a petition for an evidentiary hearing to explore the operations of Albuquerque, New Mexico, television station KGGM, which could lead to important precedents for programming obligations of commercial t.v. stations to minority groups in their broadcast area. Indians, and other groups, alleged that the station had failed to serve the needs of the area's minority populations with locally developed programs, failed to provide equal employment opportunities, and other claims. The case represented the first time the FCC had ever designated a commercial t.v. station for a hearing on the basis of a citizen petition to deny license renewal charging racial discrimination.

August. With the opening of the new school year, the antiquated facilities at Acomita, New Mexico, were replaced with the realization of a beautiful new school at the Acoma Pueblo, named "Sky City." The plant is one of open design and accomodates a program for children grades K through eight.

September 15. The Department of Housing and Urban Development (HUD) announced the creation of a HUD Task Force on Indian Housing Programs which would recommend "policy alternatives" and "field organization to best support Indian programs."

In early October, U.S. Senator James Abourezk dropped consideration of S.B. 1328 and promised support of S.B. 2010, introduced by Senator Henry Jackson, at the request of the National Congress of American Indians, which would repeal Public Law 83-280.

A federal court test loomed ahead in October for the Ute (Utah) tribe's attempt to assert jurisdiction over non-Indian individuals and towns. Despite the tension and resentment raised by the issue, there had been no incidents. The Ute's wish to apply tribal law in an area which includes the towns of Duchesne, Roosevelt, Myton, Neola and Altamont. The towns have a combined population of about 4,000 and are encompassed by the 1.3 million acre Unitah and Ouray Indian Reservation. Tribal Chairman Lester Chapoose was quoted as saying, "We will no longer stand idly by and watch our resources ruined, our people humiliated and our competency questioned." The 1600 member tribe feels that if state officials can prosecute Indians who violate state laws off the reservation, the Utes can prosecute non-Indians who violate Ute laws on or affecting the reservation. A tribal code claiming civil and criminal jurisdiction over all lands, including exterior boundaries, went into effect September 15. Indians in two other states proceeded to follow a similar course of action.

October. The Fund for the Improvement of Post-Secondary Education (FIPSE) awarded the Mississippi Band of Choctaw Indians, Philadelphia, Miss. $29,341 to extend educational services to tribal members by providing accredited college course work on the reservation and in nearby post-secondary institutions. This Indian-controlled project also provided counseling and tutoring for individuals who had never been to college.

October 30. The Indian Pueblo Cultural Center was dedicated with the start of construction of the $2 million center on the Indian school campus at Albuquerque, New Mexico. The center, with 49,000 square feet of floor space on three levels, will be opened in the summer of 1976 as a showcase for the Indian culture, history and tradition. Senator Joseph Montoya said the fact that the eighteen pueblos of New Mexico had banded together to make the center a reality will enable others "to appreciate the ancient and still living art and music and stories and philosophy of the people of this great river valley." The Senator reminded the audience that he had been a friend and neighbor of the pueblo Indian people all his life.

November. Dr. Frank Clarke, a Hopi and Hualapai Indian who had been in private practice for twenty years joined the Albuquerque, New Mexico, Indian Hospital. He is the past president of the Association of American Indian Physicians and has been active in the recruitment of Indian youths for the medical field. During the Korean War, Dr. Clarke saw active duty as a Naval medical officer. Previous to his Albuquerque appointment, he had been working in a volunteer capacity at the hospital and as a consultant to mental health and alcoholism programs serving Indian groups, after having been a family practitioner in Woodlake, California.

The New Mexico state appropriation to the world-famed Inter-Tribal Indian Ceremonial Association was the center of controversy in that state in mid-November. The State

Commission on Indian Affairs, which met at Dulce, New Mexico, said that a report on how the appropriation was spent was inadequate. The commission adopted a motion by vice-chairman Joe Baca, a Santa Clara-Jicarilla Apache, which called for money now being appropriated to the Inter-Tribal Ceremonial to be henceforth directed to the commission for Indian arts and crafts. Eight of the ten commission members are Indians under the restructuring voted by the 1975 state legislature.

November. Dr. William Demmert, deputy commissioner for Indian education, spoke at an Oklahoma City educational convention and stated, "Different parts of the Indian community need different things. The Navajos and the Eskimos for instance, are very concerned about the survival of their culture." Demmert, who is half Sioux and half Tlingit, (a tribe in southeast Alaska), said the larger the percentage of Indian students in a school, the more Indians need to be on the local school board. He added that if an Indian community is unhappy with a federally controlled school, it should establish its own school as an alternative. Demmert said Indian students need a special emphasis on their culture in the schools. "If I hadn't grown up strongly in my tribe and in my culture, I don't know where I'd be today," he said.

November 20. The U.S. Interior Department Appropriation Bill, which included multi-million dollar expenditures for Indian-related programs and projects, went to the full Senate floor for expected approval. Included were not only the traditional Johnson-O'Malley school funds, but long needed improvements at hospitals around the Indian nations and for the Navajo Community College and other university training programs.

November 21. A century-old land dispute between the Hopi and Navajo tribes ended with the receipt of a memorandum by the Bureau of Land Management from the Navajos in preparation for the movement of about sixty Navajo families along with 12,000 sheep from disputed joint-use land to the isolated 250,000 acre House Rock Valley near the Arizona-Utah border. A proposed Navajo plan calls for the building of schools, clinics and commercial establishments to take care of the needs of the new Indian residents. Funds for the resettlement, including money for construction of new homes, were provided under a recently enacted law.

The All-Indian Pueblo Council announced on November 22 that it planned to file a complaint with the Equal Employment Opportunity Commission (EEOC), calling for an investigation into hiring practices by the state of New Mexico. Council Chairman Delfin J. Lovato called the state employment situation for Indians as "a total lack of opportunity for Indian people." The complaint followed a report on Indian employment prepared by the New Mexico Advisory Committee to the U.S. Commission on Civil Rights, which showed a virtual lack of Indians in other than routine jobs of the lowest paying nature, and even then a mere two hundred plus.

November 27. The director of the California Tribal Chairmen's Association, Jim Wounded Hawk Hawkins, concluded that Indians had a "tinge of guilt," about selling Manhattan Island in 1626 for $24 worth of beads and trinkets. The association had been trying for a week to collect money from 6,000 members to aid financially beleagured and virtually bankrupt New York City. No Indian had even donated a single dollar!

In December, the Navajo Tribal Council was considering a five year lease with Southern Utah Industries to operate a shirt plant in the former Fairchild Semi-Conductor plant at Shiprock, New Mexico. The plant was to hire about 400 persons who had been left jobless when the former tenants moved out after an AIM occupation of the plant. The lease called for a reduction in its annual rent, for every Navajo employed at the plant. The lease agreement also called for financial protection for the firm in case of another takeover.

In a December 3rd press release it was noted by the American Indian Law Center's Thelma Stiffarm, that, "only 150 Indians have graduated from law schools across the country so far, and 122 are enrolled at thirty-nine schools. The need for Indian Lawyers is great today with Indian interests in water, oil and gas.''

Late December. The U.S. Army, after a new study conducted by them, denied that Cavalry men engaged in "deliberate, intentional shooting of helpless persons at Wounded Knee, South Dakota eighty-five years ago.''

A December released study made by the Federal Indian Domestic Assistance Program revealed that of 1200 federal domestic assistance programs last year, Indian tribes only took part in seventy-eight. Phil Lujan, of the Indian Law Center said, "Of all the money appropriated, only .004 per cent of it went to Indian programs.''

In December, as the year ended, the New Mexico Highway Department refused to talk about twenty-one miles of Interstate Highway proposed reconstruction for completing I-25 between Santa Fe and Albuquerque, New Mexico. The unusual influence of a small traditionalist pueblo on the Rio Grande over the state's largest agency is because the Santo Domingo pueblo controls the right-of-way for two-thirds of the route. It would cost a fortune to go around the pueblo grant land or confine the highway in the present right-of-way. The Department cannot condemn the land, as it could that of a private citizen, without using a 1926 federal law that is in the process of being repealed by Congress. Santo Domingo Pueblo Council Secretary Benny Atencio authorized a survey line to be run along the existing highway but said, "all we are asking is that negotiations be private." He said that the tribe is willing to discuss right of way and, "we have been working on this for several years." State Representative Edward Lopez said that an alternate route would add nine miles to the highway and cost an additional $40 million.

1976   In January, during the winter session, the Navajo Tribal Council again took up the hotly disputed El Paso Natural Gas Company coal lease question postponed from the fall session. The issue involved extending an El Paso coal lease on the reservation which is tied in with plans for a proposed coal gasification plant. Tribal Chairman Peter

MacDonald said, "Economic development is necessary but it should not be done at the expense of our treaty or sovereign status."

On January 9, the ABC-TV network presented I WILL FIGHT NO MORE FOREVER, the story of the last tribe of American Indians to fight confinement on a reservation.

AMERICAN HORSE

The chief of the Oglala Sioux who signed the treaty in 1887 whereby the Sioux reservation in the Dakotas was lowered to one-half of its former size. The bare majority of his people siding with his decision became restive with the news of the death of Sitting Bull. This is the tribe alleged to have led the Ghost Dance Uprising. Their withdrawal from the council and preparations to fight the Government caused much concern for a time. Chief American Horse ultimately prevailed upon his braves to accept the terms of the treaty. Several years later, in 1891, he led a delegation from the Pine Ridge Reservation to the nation's capital where they successfully obtained improved treatment and living rations.

BLACK HAWK

A famed leader of the Sauk and Fox Indians, and commander in the Black Hawk War of 1832. Legend states that he was born in 1767, a warrior at fifteen and had taken his first scalp by the time he had reached the tender age of seventeen. Black Hawk did not recognize an 1812 treaty under which his tribe was to move to the west bank of the Mississippi, because he claimed it had been arrived at by deception and fraud. The treaty may have played a part in his decision to take his Sauk followers and fight for the British during the War of 1812, whereas his fellow chieftan, Keokuk, and his group stayed and fought with the Americans. It is known that the treaty played a part in his decision to go to war in 1832, and it is noteworthy that one of his adversaries, Abraham Lincoln, was destined later to become president of the United States. With the defeat of the Indians, Black Hawk fled northward, where he was captured and imprisoned in Virginia. He died after his release from prison in 1838. His stolen body was carried to St. Louis, and later his bones were made into a skeleton which sparked a controversy with the Indians led by his son. The bones were destroyed when the Burlington Geographical and Historical Society's museum in Iowa caught fire in 1855.

JOSEPH BRANDT

(Thayandanega) of the Mohawks was educated in English mission schools and commissioned a colonel in the British Army. He was a principal leader, holding the Six Nations loyal in their allegiance with England during the Revolutionary War. He later became quite wealthy. While his father was a full blooded Mohawk chief, there are claims that his mother was half white. After the death of Brandt's father, his mother remarried a man by the name of Brandt, whose name he took. His sister, Molly, was married to Sir William Johnson, and the young boy went to live in her home. He took part in many Revolutionary War battles, including the massacre of the whites at Cherry Valley. As testimony to the English appreciation of Brandt's services, they continued to pay him half his colonel's pay in retirement and granted him a vast tract of land six miles wide along the Grand River in Ontario, Canada. He is credited with having translated the Bible into the Mohawk language before he died in November, 1807.

BRIGHT EYES

Susette La Flesche, daughter of a former Chief of the Omaha Indians, noted for her work to improve conditions for Indians living on reservations. While working with the Ponca who had been removed from the Omaha reservation to other Indian territory, she cared for the sick and dying. The situation made national headlines in newspapers, and public interest was aroused to the point that the removal prompted Judge Dundy to issue his noted court decision that, "an Indian is a person." She later married a white man, Henry Tribbles, who in 1902 wrote the book, Buckskin and Blanket Days, which was not published until 1957.

CHARLES CARTER

A Choctaw, he was one of the early members of the United States House of Representatives, and served in the state of Oklahoma from 1907-1927.

JESSE CHISHOLM

This Cherokee is famed for blazing the famous cattle trail from Texas through Oklahoma to railroad terminals in Kansas...which is now partly on U.S. Highway #81.

COCHISE

The famed Chiricahua Apache chief who headed the tribal upheaval against the white men in the 1870's. This wily warrior had opposed efforts to relocate the Apaches on a new reservation in New Mexico. With his force of less than two hundred soldiers he was able to keep the U.S. Army at bay for over four years, and ultimately forced the Government to concede its own virtual defeat, when it agreed to a peace with an undefeated enemy. Only then, with a new reservation created for them in Arizona, did Cochise lead in the braves. He is acknowledged to have been able to recognize the folly of having his people segregated from the white men on a reservation and pled for integration with the whites everywhere -- on the farm and in the town -- saying, "Let us be one people." Years after, when white programs had not remedied the Indian situation, white administrators remembered Cochise's plea. He died in June 1874.

CARLOS MONTEZUMA

At the age of five years, "Wasajah", which translated means "Beckoning", was taken by the Pima Indians during an 1871 raid on the Apaches in Arizona. Later he was sold for the price of a horse, about $30, to a white prospector, Charles Gentile, who befriended him and placed him in schools in Chicago. After graduating from the University of Illinois and the Chicago Medical School, he served as an instructor in the Post Graduate Medical School and other medical schools in the Chicago area where he practiced. Later he served as a physician at a number of Indian posts. During his lifetime, he tried to stimulate Indian interest and pride and to secure white help for them. He died at Fort McDowell, Arizona in 1923, with some accounts giving the month as January, and others February.

CORNPLANTER

Cornplanter was the noted Seneca chief, also known as John O'Bail, son of an Indian woman and a white father. He was born some time in the period of the 1770's and is reputed to have died in 1836. The tale goes that when the Indian grew up he longed to see the father he did not know as a child. After his marriage he went to see the elder O'Bail and introduced himself. The white man gave him food and was kind but did not offer him anything to eat on his return journey to the Indian village. During the American Revolution, the Indian fought for the English and captured his white parent. He urged his father to return with him and vowed to keep him safe and satisfied, but when the white man refused, Cornplanter saw that he was released and returned to his home. Some versions of the story state that the senior O'Bail was captured by a raiding party before the Revolution, but the essential ingredients of the story are the same. Later, Cornplanter was given a pardon for his participation in the War for Independence and showed his appreciation by offering to serve in the War of 1812. He was refused due to his age, but his son, Henry, did perform valiant service and rose to become a major in the United States Army. He was a man of peace after warring, and many treaties bear his mark, attesting to his love for the white man and desire for peace after having warred against the settlements in his earlier years. He died a man most respected by his white contemporaries, including Generals Washington and Wayne.

CRAZY HORSE

One of the most famous of Indian chiefs, this Oglala Sioux's name was misunderstood and wrongly translated by the white men, who should have properly called him, "His Horse Is Crazy". This Indian was with Sitting Bull when the Sioux were forced into war in 1875 to resist the inroads of gold miners who ventured into the Black Hills. He led his men in the Custer debacle the following year. He was so relentlessly chased by the U.S. Cavalry who wished to avenge their defeat at Little Big Horn, that in the early part of 1877 he capitulated with some 2,000 followers. He was accused of trying to escape and put in prison. Contrary to the usual white versions of the story, one old chief reported that Crazy Horse was taken from his cell at Fort Robinson by two soldiers or Indian traitors. Then, held by the two men, he was killed by a soldier who ran a bayonette through his back into his kidney. Crazy Horse is alleged never to have taken a scalp from his enemies when he killed them. A monument to his memory is being carved in the Black Hills close to Mount Rushmore, financed by private funds and scheduled to be completed in 1980.

GERONIMO

There are conflicting stories about this noted medicine man, prophet and chief of the Chiricahua Apaches of Arizona. Some are favorable and some are damning. His true name was "Goyathlay", or "One Who Yawns", but he was generally called Geronimo, which was the Spanish name for Jerome. This wily chief was born sometime around 1834 near old Fort Tularosa in New Mexico. When Cochise made peace with the federal government and agreed to go to a reservation near San Carlos in Arizona, Geronimo and some of his men decamped into Old Mexico. Later they were captured and placed on the reservation, but when a dispute arose over irrigation needs, and the government refused to help the Indians, Geronimo once more took to the warpath for a short time before again surrendering. Another outbreak came in 1884 when the federal government attempted to stop the making of intoxicating brews by the Indians. Raids were made on white settlers in Arizona and New Mexico, as well as upon Mexicans in Sonora and Chihuahua. The old Indian fighter, General George A. Crook, began a campaign in March, 1886 to kill or quiet the annoying Apaches once and for all. Geronimo agreed to a proposal, but it was again violated. General Nelson Miles was then assigned the task of relentlessly pursuing the Indians until in August they surrendered. They were banished to Fort Sill and given hard labor for four years. Geronimo died in 1909.

L. ROSA MINOKA HILL

Dr. Hill was a member of the New York Mohawk tribe and had the honor of being the first Indian woman physician. She was noted for her many humanitarian activities.

JOSEPH

This Nez Perce chief was respected by white men for his oratory and wisdom. His Indian name was Hinmaton-yalatkit, which meant "Thunder Coming from the Water over the Land". When his tribe, which had always been cordial to the white people, revolted against the Treaty of 1863 (which permitted settlers to obtain possession of the Wallawa Valley in Idaho), they were told that they would have to pay a further penalty and be forced to live on a reservation. The Nez Perce ignored the order, and in 1877 the government agent insisted that they must report to their new lands near Fort Lapwai, Idaho. Chief Joseph once more chose to ignore the order, and a battle with the whites ensued on June 6, 1877, at White Bird Canyon, close to the Salmon River in Idaho. He was defeated by the federal troops but managed to escape with most of his warriors to lead the men, women and children of his tribe toward a destination in Canada. For over two months and with many skirmishes, he fended off several government forces which attempted to surround him. He managed to elude and out-general the white commanders with their superior weaponry and supplies. His campaign was a remarkable example of strategy, against superior odds. When he supposed he had gained escape he stopped to rest his tired people on what he thought was Canadian soil, but which turned out to be in the Bear Paw Mountains in Montana. (Hot debates remain as to whether he was inside Canada, a few miles away, or a day's journey; the fact remains, he was captured.) He surrendered only after eluding three U.S. Army groups. A fourth, under General Miles, surrounded his men and poured howitzer and Gatling gun shells at them for five days. On October 5, 1877, he was forced to surrender. Joseph was made to go to Oklahoma as a captive. Ultimately he and his followers were granted permission to resettle on the Colville Reservation in Washington, where Joseph died on September 21, 1904. A white marble monument erected to his honor can be viewed in the cemetary at Nespelim, Washington, where he was buried.

KEOKUK

This Sauk Indian leader was born in Illinois, about the year 1770. His name meant "Watchful Fox". He was not one of the fortunate group who inherited chieftanship by birth, but gained the honor as a result of his deft leadership, the fire of his strong personality and his remarkable

oratory. With the Americans he was noted more for his wisdom and talk-
ing ability than for being a warrior. During the War of 1812, when the
Sauk and Fox tribes divided their loyalties, and one group followed Chief
Black Hawk, Keokuk remained loyal to the Americans, while not actually
fighting in the conflict. His desire was to lead in peace and not in war.
Later in 1832, he again refused to join in warfare during the Black Hawk
War. He is most noted for the skillful manner in which he debated successfully with government officials to firmly establish his tribe's claim
to what is now the State of Iowa. Although he was buried in Kansas when
he died in 1848, he was subsequently reinterred in 1883 in Keokuk, Iowa,
where a monument was built to his memory. A bronze bust of this great
Indian leader may be viewed in the United States Senate in Washington,
D.C., and the country further honored him and his people by placing his
likeness on an old issue of paper currency.

LITTLE TURTLE

This famous Miami Indian chief was born in 1752 at a place on the
Eel River near today's Fort Wayne, Indiana. His prowess was quickly
recognized, and he became a chief at an unusually early age. His was the
mind behind the strategy which defeated General Harmar in 1780 when
settlers agitated for the opening of the Northwest Territory, with consequent bloodshed. The victory was short-lived, for within five years "Mad"
Anthony Wayne had decisively defeated the Indians, who were forced to
sign a treaty of peace. Little Turtle's words at that unhappy moment are
alleged to have been, "I am the last to sign this treaty and will be the last
to break it." It is noteworthy that he kept his word, for when Tecumseh
went on the warpath in the War of 1812, Little Turtle did not join forces
with him. An interesting event was his trip to the nation's capital in Washington in 1797, where he met the famed Polish general who had aided the
colonists during the American Revolution, General Thaddeus Kosciusko,
who was so intrigued with Little Turtle that he gave him his prized pair
of hand guns. At that time the reknowned artist, Gilbert Stuart, painted
his portrait. Little Turtle died in 1812.

JAMES (or JOHN) LOGAN

This famous Iroquois orator and chief was born in 1725 near Sham-
okin, Pennsylvania. His Indian name was Tahgahjute, which translated
meant, "His Eyelashes Stick Out, or Above!" He honored a white friend
by adopting the name of James Logan, after William Penn's secretary.
Logan comes down to us in historical annals because of his famed 1744
speech in Circleville, Ohio, delivered after white men had murdered many
of his followers, including his wife and all members of his family. This

caused his understandable fight to revenge his losses by warring against
the colonist culprits. He was killed by a nephew in 1780 and is buried in
Fort Hill Cemetery, Auburn, New York, where a monument was subsequently erected to his memory.

MASSASOIT

Undoubtedly the early northeastern colonists owed much to this
great chief of the Wampanoag tribe, whose domain included what is now
Massachusetts and Rhode Island. The grand sachem's real name was
"Wasamegin", which translated meant "Yellow Feather". Without the
help of this powerful chieftain, who entered into a treaty of peace with the
white men and bequeathed large amounts of land to them, the colonists
would have perished. It was he who taught the white men how to plant and
cook. It was he who had his people share their food and lore of living with
the whites. He was grateful to the English for having saved his life when
he was dangerously ill in the winter of 1623. He was a peacemaker when
conflicts of understanding arose between the Indians who did not compre-
hend that they no longer had possession and rights to lands which were
given or sold to them, and the whites who wanted them off the land. His
death in 1661 was a severe loss for the whites. He left behind two sons,
Wamsutta and Metacomet (Philip).

MILLY

Analagous to the story of John Smith and Pocahontas is that of the
American, Duncan McKrimmon, and Milly, a beautiful daughter of a Seminole chief. The account passed down to us is that the American had been
captured in 1817 and ordered to be burned at the stake. When the fire
was lighted, Milly dropped to her feet before her father and cried for the
sparing of the white man's life, under threat of joining the white man in
the flames. The aging chief, Hillis Hadjo, acceded to her request, and
instead sold the American to the Spaniards as a slave. The story does
not end there. Some time later, Milly was unfortunate enough to be captured by American soldiers, and McKrimmon, who was then a free man,
succeeded in obtaining her release. His offer to marry her was misunderstood by the Indian maid who thought he was only doing it out of gratitude for having saved his life, so she refused and eventually married an
Indian.

OSCEOLA

Osceola was a Seminole Indian chief who was born about 1803, in
Creek territory, Florida. He became a chief at the early age of thirty-two

years, not by the traditional route of inheritance, but from common recognition of his leadership qualities. He came to the fore as a leader when
the federal government commenced the difficult attempt to gather up the
Seminoles and put them on a reservation in Oklahoma. During the fighting
in the swampy Everglades of Florida, Osceola constantly made fools of the
Americans by outwitting them. Overtures for peace were sent to him,
and he agreed to attend a meeting under a flag of truce. He was knocked
on the head, tied up and tossed into a dungeon by a calloused and dishonest
general. This breaking of faith caused a furor in the country when it was
made public. Osceola died in January, 1838 in the Fort Moultrie, Florida
prison, a broken-hearted man.

PHILIP

This son of the famous Massasoit was the great chief of the Wampanoag tribe. While his Indian name was Metacomet, the English called
him King Philip. Considered to be the most outstanding leader of the New
England tribes, he is best known as the director of King Philip's War,
which took place in the years 1675 to 1676. It was the worst war in the
annals of the New England colonists, but more devastating for the Indians.
The turning point of that war took place on August 12, 1676, at a white
fortress in the swamps of Rhode Island, where the Indians were soundly
defeated and their leader killed in the battle. King Philip was one of a
small group of Indians who were able to visualize the inherent possibilities for Indian resistance to white settlements by joining forces in a federated Indian tribes reaction campaign.

POCAHONTAS

Pocahontas, also known as Matoaka (Matsoaks'ats), daughter of
Powhatan, went to London as the wife of John Rolfe. She had her portrait
painted in April 1616 when she was but twenty-one, but unable to withstand
the English climate, she soon died -- presumably from tuberculosis.
Translated, her name means "lively one". (The romantic episode relating
how she saved the life of Captain John Smith of the Jamestown colony is
suspected to be a myth by many researchers, although history has a ten-
dency to accept it.)

PONTIAC

The exact date of the birth of this bold leader is not known, but is
variously given as 1720-1725. He was born of an Ottawa mother and a
Chippewa father. He was one of a number of Indian chiefs who had formulated beliefs that the English policy toward the red men was worse than

that of the French. He was acknowledged to be highly intelligent, realistic, qualified and commanding in presence -- all the qualities attributed to any leader. Pontiac was influenced by an Indian mystic and the Seneca tribes' desire to attack the English at Fort Detroit. He accepted the Seneca plan of conspiracy to drive the English back by attacking them at several points, thus destroying his foe's strength in the West. At a ground council meeting in the Detroit River in April, 1763, plans were laid for the assault. The initial plan was betrayed to the British commander, with the result that the Indians were repulsed, perhaps an omen of the ultimate end' for after a spring, summer and autumn of intense warfare, Pontiac started to lose his men, and snow began to fall. He wrote letters to the English and virtually sued for peace, after finding from a winter of travel to other tribes that no one had stomach for further fighting. The treaty was signed in April 1765. Pontiac was assassinated by a Peoria Indian, Black Dog, while doing some peaceful trading in 1769.

POPE

El Pope was the San Juan Pueblo Indian generally credited as being the leader of the great Pueblo Rebellion against the Spanish on August 10, 1680. Pope was one of almost fifty Pueblo medicine men rudely brought into Santa Fe by a new governor, determined to crush the Indians for refusing to give more than lip service to Christianity and instead continuing their own religious practices secretly despite threats of the punishment. Pope was fortunate in not losing his life, as did some of the Indians accused of witchcraft. After being released from prison, Pope went into hiding at Taos Pueblo where he planned and organized the all-Pueblo rebellion. A tight espionage system of runners was created to secretly convey messages to all the Pueblos. Originally the attack was planned for August 13, but fearing a news leak, Pope ordered the date of attack to be moved up to August 10. About 500 of the 2,500 Spaniards living in the province were killed, and after a few days the remainder broke out of Santa Fe and fled south to El Paso, Texas. The Indians proceeded to remove and burn everything Spanish, killed all animals, razed the churches, and even destroyed fruits and vegetables. The old Pueblo way of life was restored. Pope traveled from one pueblo to another and was received with great honors, but rivalry and jealousy were natural responses to his despotic conduct. He was deposed for a number of years but was reinstalled in 1688 shortly before his death. For a few years more, the Pueblos ran things as they wished, during which time there were plagues, retreats of some Pueblos and Apache and Ute allies to more remote mountain places, and repeated unsuccessful attempts by the Spanish to recapture the province. In 1692, after four years of sporadic and brutal fighting, the Europeans under General DeVargas were successful. Although peace was attained, the Pueblos lost faith in Spanish Christianity and pursued their old ways and dances secretly in their kivas. An interesting rebuttal of this accepted account is given by Fray Angelico Chavez, a Franciscan friar and writer with a flair for history, who claims that the leader of the revolt was actually a giant black mulatto with yellow eyes. Fray Chavez claims that he noted this while pouring over archives of the period, and claims reinforcement from Indian legends and accounts given by prisoners during the seige of Santa Fe.

RED CLOUD

This most famous chief of the largest group of the Dakota nation, the Oglala Sioux, was born in 1822. When the government started to con-struct a road in 1865 to lead from Fort Laramie, Wyoming, to the gold fields of Montana -- a road that would ruin the prime buffalo hunting grounds of the Indians -- he protested in vain. For tribal preservation, he gath-ered about 2,000 fighters in December 1866 and destroyed a body of troops adjacent to Fort Kearney. This forced the government to retract its pro-grammed road, and thereafter Red Cloud gave the white men no more trouble, despite the forced cecession of the "Black Hills" of South Dakota. It is significant to note that Red Cloud did not join in the Sioux war of 1876. This great Indian general, statesman, orator and pragmatic Sioux leader died in 1909. The town of Red Cloud, Nebraska, is named after him, and properly so, for it was Sioux territory.

SACAGAWEA

This Shoshone Indian woman is probably the second most famous maiden of her race, with only Pocohantas possibly rated ahead by story writers. She was born around 1787 and was known to white people as the "Bird Woman". She was captured by an Hidatsa, sold to a Missouri Man-dan Indian and ultimately to a French Canadian fur trader by the name of Toussaint Charbonneau. The fur trader was hired by the Lewis and Clark expedition as an interpreter. Despite having a new-born child, Sacagawea went along, for she longed to visit her own people. Ultimately she became a guide for the explorers. Her role as ambassador of peace and friend was stated by Clark: "She reconciles all the Indians to our friendly tribes. A woman with a party of men is a token of peace." After crossing the plains, the expedition was faced with the task of climbing the perilious and lofty snow-capped Rocky Mountains, without horses and nearly out of pro-visions. Going on ahead of the main group, Merriweather Lewis fortunately contacted a group of Shoshone Indians who agreed to return to the main camp with him. At Three Forks, Montana, our Indian heroine was finally introduced to her own people and "danced with joy." She learned that her brother had advanced to become chief of her people. After the reunion with her people, it was easy for the party to secure help and horses with which the expedition was able to attain their objective of reaching the Pacific Ocean and map the intervening land. On returning to their Mandan village, Sacagawea's husband was paid for his services' and she remained with him. Their child was educated by the government by virtue of Clark's interest. While some historians credit Sacagawea's death around 1812 at the age of 24 or 25, based upon reports from a fur trader, there are other claims that she was discovered by a missionary in 1875 and that she actually died in Wyoming on April 9, 1884 -- almost one hundred years old.

SAMOSET

This Pemaquid Indian sagamore was the first Indian to welcome the Pilgrims when they touched land on Cape Cod, Massachusetts, in 1620. He is alleged to have used English, saying, "Welcome, Englishmen!" which he is presumed to have learned from earlier contacts with white fishermen. Samoset is the one who introduced the Pilgrim Fathers to their great benefactor, Massasoit. Samoset assisted in the arrangements for signing the first deed between the Pilgrims and the Indians, which covered about 12,000 acres of land sold to John Brown of New Harbor, Maine.

SEQUOYA

This is the Cherokee Indian born in Taskigi, Tennessee, in 1760, to whom the members of his tribe can point with particular pride, for he is the inventor of Cherokee syllabary. The Indians called him "Siwayi"; however, he was also known as George Gist, the name of his white father. At an early age he showed his creative qualities as a "natural" at mechanical things and an expert in silverworking; but unfortunately he was permanently crippled as a result of a hunting accident. Despite his never having gone to formal schools and lacking the ability to speak or understand English, he was a most astute observer. He noted the way the white people could communicate and the importance of reading, writing and the use of the printing press. He began to search for a way to make these arts available to his people. He studied the English letters in the church school books and soon was involved in his quest. His first approach was via a picture-word technique, but after passing 1,000 he abandoned this as too cumbersome. His home and all his notes were burned when his tribesmen suspected him of practicing witchcraft and drove him out of his Cherokee village for safer climes of Arkansas. In 1821, after twelve years of labor, he was satisfied with a reduction of his alphabet from 200 characters to 85. The Cherokee language is difficult to learn; one almost has to grow

up with it. Sequoya's alphabet was a combination of English characters
with different sounds and many of his own ideas. He returned to his eastern Cherokee village with a message from the western Cherokees addressed
to the tribal elders. They listened to his story, studied his efforts and
gave their approval to the alphabet which was to revolutionize Cherokee
education. It was quickly seized upon by the members of the tribe, and it
was not long before reading and writing their own language became general.
Soon their newspaper and the Bible were also being printed in the syllabary
of Sequoya. This brilliant Indian was the first man to receive the honor of
a silver medal and a lifetime pension from the Cherokee Legislature. He
later went searching for a lost group of Cherokees, possibly amalgamated
with other tribes. He sought to trace speech patterns of Indian tribes in
the Southwest. The exact time and place of his death is unknown. Some
say he died in old Mexico; others mention the possibility of a remote grave
in the mountains at Snyder, Texas, but all appear to accept a death date
of 1843. Cherokee syllabary is said to be fast becoming lost because the
Indian youth are using English rather than the demanding and graceful
Cherokee language. There are many drawers of documents written in
Cherokee existing in the Smithsonian Library; but many others are lost
forever, having been tossed aside and discarded by thoughtless Indians.

SITTING BULL

Tatanka Iyotake, known to the white men as Sitting Bull, was the
most famous chief of the Hunkapapa, or Western (Teton) Sioux. He was
the leader of the largest grouping of Plains Indians in history. Born in
South Dakota in 1831, even as a child he was remarkable, commanding
the attention and respect of his people. He was a shaman, and his visions
were extraordinary. He believed that he was given divine powers to lead
and protect his people. Despite the fact that many northern Plains tribes
gave up the battle against the white man and federal regulations, he was
battling them virtually all the time after 1866. The government ordered
all Sioux to go to reservations in December of 1875 and be there by the
end of January, lest they be judged hostile; and when the Sioux couldn't
meet this ridiculous time table, they were attacked by troops under the
command of General Crook. The Indians scattered and ultimately Sitting
Bull and his followers managed to get to their camp on the Rosebud River.
The spring of 1876 found approximately 3,000 Sioux and Cheyenne center-
ing their presence and hopes for survival around the acknowledged chief
of chiefs. It became evident to this extraordinary leader that a battle for
their very life was shaping. In June 1876, he enacted the Sun Dance which
he said would give him the knowledge of how to lead his followers in the
challenge which lay ahead. As a preliminary, he gave away 100 pieces
of skin which he took from his shoulders and arms. Bleeding freely after

that blood-letting part of the ceremony, he proceeded to dance all day and night until noon of the second day, when, almost unconscious, he had the sought-for vision. He proclaimed that he witnessed many white soldiers tumbling upside down from the sky who would do battle with his people, but that the Great Spirit would take care of his people. He did not have long to wait, for on June 16, 1,000 Indian warriors under Crazy Horse met 1,300 federal troopers under General Crook at the Battle of the Rosebud. Despite fatigue from his Sun Dance ordeal, Sitting Bull nonetheless managed to be present to inspire his warriors. After an all-day battle, the federal troops gave ground, suffering huge losses. It was not the end, and Sitting Bull knew it. On June 25, the battle which has gone down in history as Custer's Last Stand occurred, without prior plans to trap the white forces. Actually, it was a defensive action. The story does not end here. The army continually pressured the Indians after their defeat, and, unable to avoid the loss of his traditional hunting grounds in the Dakotas, Sitting Bull managed to elude his oppressors in Canada where he vainly sought refuge. The army and U.S. Commissioners urged him to return, but only when the Indians were on the edge of starvation did he accept a "pardon" on July 19, 1881. He was kept a virtual prisoner at Fort Randall for two years, during which time he was admired by many whites, but at the same time he incurred the hatred of the agent and rival chiefs. He accompanied the Buffalo Bill Wild West Show for a time in the 1880's, also a period in which the ill blood with the Indian agent, James McLaughlin, was kept alive. With the Ghost Dance Movement spreading to the Indian reservations in the Dakota territory, the feud between Sitting Bull and the Indian agent became white hot. Although the Indian chief had given a lack-luster endorsement to the Ghost Dance philosophy, he kept somewhat aloof despite a December invitation to go to the Pine Ridge area. McLaughlin seized upon the invitation as a pretext for imprisoning his foe, and sent a number of Indian police to place Sitting Bull under arrest. A number of his close warriors sought to avoid his capture, and scuffling broke out. In the melee, Indian Police Sergeants Bullhead and Red Tomahawk killed the chief along with his son and six others. Sitting Bull was initially buried in Fort Yates, North Dakota, but in 1953 his body was exhumed and car- ried to Mobridge, South Dakota where a granite shaft was subsequently erected to his honor and memory. He left behind a series of autobiograph- ical sketches in which he personally recounted his life.

SQUANTO

Squanto, savior of the Plymouth Colony, made an early display of unselfish conduct in his relations with the settlers. He is considered to be the reason that the colony survived that terrible first winter in the New World. Historians can't seem to find a reason for his assistance, because he had been inhumanly treated by earlier English explorers, captured and sold as a slave. He subsequently escaped from these "ugly Englishmen" and on his return to his village found that the whole tribe had been the victims of another English unwelcome gift package to the new world -- small pox. After being so helpful at Plymouth, Squanto died about two years later from the "fever".

TECUMSEH

Tecumseh, who was a great Shawnee Chief, envisioned the unity of the Indian tribes and spent much of his time traveling to attain his goal of a great Indian confederacy. The Creeks, not surprisingly, were divided; the Chickasaws tarried; the Cherokees and the Choctaws refused to go to war. Despite this, many of the tribes commenced war against the white man until General Andrew Jackson defeated them in 1814. At a later date, the Seminoles took up the war cry, and Jackson was obliged to return and do battle with the warring tribes. For some reason not clearly understood, one tribe at a time fought the whites, evidently failing to understand the value of joint effort. The Seminoles were led by Osceola, but they, too, eventually succumbed, although some elements held out in the swamps of Florida. Tecumseh's half-brother, Elkswatawa, was a mystic known as the Prophet, who went about teaching his people a philosophy of America for Americans, be loyal to tribal traditions, fight for them if necessary, etc. The two formed a sort of early socialistic, or utopian village, where alcohol was banned, hard work was a virtue, and thriftiness was praised. Tecumseh's "I Have a Dream" speech was that of an Indian United States buffering the Americans from the British on the North and the Spanish on the South. Tecumseh died in the battle of the Thames River, against General Harrison, on October 5, 1813.

CLARENCE ACOYA

Clarence Acoya, a Laguna Indian, attended the University of New Mexico, worked for the B. F. Hutton Company as a representative, was treasurer of his tribe and formerly the Executive Director of the New Mexico Commission on Indian Affairs. Director, Ford Foundation Fund of the National Congress of American Indians. Veteran. Now Assistant to Commissioner of B.I.A.

DOLLY SMITH AKERS

Mrs. Akers, an Assiniboine Indian, was the only woman elected first to her tribal council and then later to become its chairman. She entered politics desirous of assisting her people during the depression, and in 1932 was elected to the Montana State legislature, the only woman lawmaker and first of her race and sex so honored.

MANUEL ARCHULETA

Manuel Archuleta is a San Juan Pueblo Indain married to Alyce Pino from the Laguna Pueblo. Always interested in the Indian chants, he used his meagre income to buy a small portable recorder with which he started to preserve the authentic Indian tribal songs, stories and music. From this hobby came Tom-Tom records, affording the serious student an opportunity to have his own library of Indian music.

LOUIS W. BALLARD

Born July 8, 1931, on an Indian reservation in Oklahoma, he attended Bacone College, the University of Tulsa, and Oklahoma University; and from these studies he had received a Master's degree in music, made possible through an F. B. Parriott Fellowship. He is of Cherokee-Sioux parents. He wrote the first modern American Indian ballet, "Koshare", which premiered in major U.S. cities in 1967 when it was performed by the Harkness Ballet troup, after the World Premier in Barcelona, Spain, in May 1960, at the Liceo Theatre. He also composed the original ballet, "The Four Moons", which highlighted Oklahoma's 60th Anniversary of Statehood celebrations in 1967. In September 1969, he was awarded the first Marion Nevins MacDowell Award for a chamber ensemble composition, "Ritmo Indio", which was performed October 3-5 at New London, Connecticut. In 1967 he was one of the seven American composers to receive a grant from the National Endowment for the Arts. He is a music curriculum specialist at the Institute of American Indian Arts, Santa Fe, New Mexico.

DENNIS BANKS

National Field Director of AIM, a member of the small group that formed the American Indian Movement, which initially focused its activities on the urban Indian, he quickly moved to the top posts. Convicted by an all white jury in mid-August, 1975, for rioting and assault in connection with the burning of the Custer, South Dakota, courthouse in 1973, he subsequently "went underground." His many friends and supporters recognize him as a man who picked up his responsibilities as a leader of his people when his leadership was needed. He was wounded at Wounded Knee, 1973.

JOHN BELINDO

This Navajo-Kiowa is the Executive Director of the National Congress of American Indians. He was formerly a columnist for the Daily Oklahoma Journal and a staff announcer for several Oklahoma City radio stations.

VERN BELLECOURT

This dynamic Indian personality was one of the founders of the American Indian Movement and a moving force behind many of the Indian activist show-downs in the 1972-74 period. Wounded at the second battle of Wounded Knee and charged in federal court for alleged illegal activities, the charges were dismissed in September, 1974. He was former chairman of the AIM and is presently serving on the important policy making board.

ROBERT L. BENNETT

A member of the Oneida (Wisconsin) tribe where he was born on the reservation, he was the Commissioner of Indian Affairs, having been appointed to that post by President Lyndon B. Johnson on April 27, 1966, after a long career as a civil servant in that bureau. He was the first Indian to serve in that position since General Eli Parker, President Grant's appointee from 1869 to 1871. Bennett resigned in June 1969 and served the bureau in a transition period. A lawyer by profession, he was appointed director of the American Indian Law Center at the University of New Mexico School of Law on October 9, 1969. In this new position he will coordinate and direct all the Law School's Indian programs.

BEN BLACK ELK

Perhaps the most photographed modern-day Indian, this Oglala Sioux spends his summers at the Mount Rushmore Memorial in South Dakota, where the tourists happily flock to take his photograph and pass a few words with the affable gentleman. He has appeared in many movies and documentaries, including "How the West Was Won", and he did the narration for "Legends of the Sioux" and "Tahtonka". He has been on television with regularity and was the first person to appear on Telstar. He is an authority on Indian culture, history, and lore, a high school teacher, university guest lecturer, and collaborator on many books on Indian legends, including "Black Elk Speaks", "The Sacred Pipe", and "When the Tree Flowers".

GEORGE BLUE SPRUCE

At forty-three, Dr. Blue Spruce is the nation's only full-blooded pueblo Indian dentist. As the head of the Office of Health Manpower Opportunity (HEW), this San Juan-Laguna Indian is responsible for recruitment of Indians into health professions. He served in the U.S. Navy and has received a DDS from Creighton University School of Dentistry, and a M.P.H. from the University of California at Berkeley.

LOUIS R. BRUCE

The present Indian Commissioner was appointed by the Secretary of the Interior, Walter Hickel, on August 7, 1969. Born on the Oglala Sioux Reservation at Pine Ridge, he was educated at colleges in New York, after having attended state reservation schools on the Mohawk reservation. He was a dairy farmer. He has served as the Executive Secretary of the National Congress of Indians. He was Chairman, President's Advisory Committee on American Indian Affairs; President, Arrow, Inc.; and active in Boy Scouting. He was the recipient of the American Indian Achievement Award and the Freedom Award.

CARTER CAMP

This Ponca nation Oklahoma activist Indian has truly been a warrior in his work as Chairman of the American Indian Movement since 1973, of which he was one of the founders.

ERNEST CHILDERS

Major Childers, a Creek, is one of a small band of American Indians who have received the nation's highest military award for gallantry in action above and beyond the call of duty, the Congressional Medal of Honor, for conduct in Italy during World War II. Childers enlisted in Company C, 180th Infantry Regiment, 45th Infantry, Oklahoma National Guard, composed solely of Indians. He arose through the non-commissioned officer ranks and was given a battlefield commission. After the war he decided to make the armed forces a career and subsequently attended advanced officer training schools.

MARIE CHINANA

This youthful 12-year old from Jemez pueblo early showed her artistic skill, for she was judged to be the top-place winner in the International Children's Art Show, when it was held in New York City in 1967.

WENDELL CHINO

This Mescalero Apache is the immediate past President of the National Congress of American Indian Affairs, and Chairman of two important bodies — the New Mexico Commission of Indian Affairs, and the Mescalero Apache Tribal Council. Mr. Chino has been active in pressing for improved economic and educational opportunities for his people. He was a member of the United States delegation to the Sixth Inter-American Indian Congress, held at Patzcuaro, Mexico, in April, 1968.

LOUISE ABEITA CHIWIWI

This Isleta Pueblo (New Mexico) woman showed her individuality and talents early in life, for when she was only eleven years of age, the William Morrow Publishing Company printed her book, I Am a Pueblo Indian Girl, in 1939. A sociology graduate of the University of New Mexico, she has taught in many BIA schools, and in 1965 started the first Head Start school program at her pueblo, which is located just outside of Albuquerque.

JOSEPH J. CLARK

Admiral Clark, a Cherokee Indian, was born in Pryor, Oklahoma on November 12, 1893. Subsequently he attended Willie Halsell College, Vinta, Oklahoma, and Oklahoma A & M at Stillwater and was graduated from the U.S. Naval Academy in June 1917. He served with distinction in World War I, became an instructor at the Naval Academy after that war, and was designated Naval Aviator on March 16, 1925. He served in a number of regular rotation shore and sea assignments during peacetime and World War II. During his career he received many decorations from the United States and foreign nations for his service, including the Navy Cross, Distinguished Service Medal (twice), the Legion of Merit; his last command was as Commander-in-Chief of the famous Seventh Fleet. He was transferred to the Retired List of the U.S. Navy on December 1, 1953, with the rank of Admiral, on the basis of combat citations. Since retirement, Admiral Clark has been a business executive and presently is Chairman of the Board of Hegeman Harris, Inc., in Rockefeller Center, New York.

LEON F. COOK

A member of the Chippewa tribe (Minnesota), thirty-five, he was able to overcome the handicap of not having a family and received a B.S. from St. John's University and an M.S. from the University of Minnesota School of Social Work. Besides important volunteer efforts, he worked for VISTA, OEO, and has served in a number of important federal positions. He was elected president of the National Congress of American Indians at their 28th annual convention.

VINE DELORIA, JR.

This Dakota-Yankton is an author, attorney, former executive secretary of the National Congress of American Indians, and former staff assistant of the United Scholarship Service, Denver. His first book, Custer Died for Your Sins was an immediate "best seller," and has had many printings. Later writings continued the magnetic and forceful style created in his initial endeavor.

FREDERICK DOCKSTADER

Dr. Dockstader, a Navajo, has achieved acknowledged fame in several fields of endeavor, for he is an anthropologist, author, artist, educator and silversmith. He is the Director of the Museum of the American Indian, Heye Foundation; Chairman of the Indian Arts and Crafts Board of the U.S. Department of Interior; and is a Fellow of such noted groups as the Cranbrook Institute of Science, the American Association for the Advancement of Science, and American Anthropological Association. Among his publications are The Kachina and the White Man, Indian Art in America and Indian Art in Middle America.

EDWARD P. DOZIER

Dr. Dozier from Santa Clara Pueblo has risen from an inadequate reservation school through the University of New Mexico, finally to be awarded a Ph.D. by the University of California at Los Angeles. He has attained fame as a result of his work as an anthropologist, writer and teacher. During this meteoric ascent he has been awarded many honors and study grants. His latest publication was Hano, a Tewan Indian Community in Arizona. He died in Arizona in April, 1971.

COLONEL PAT FLYNN

Colonel Flynn was a Rosebud Sioux, Marine Corps pilot in 1942, who was shot down over Japan in World War II, but escaped and returned to fight again. He was shot down over Manchuria during the Korean Conflict, captured by the Communists and made a prisoner of war.

A. E. "BUD" HAGBERG

This Eskimo is the Vice President for Traffic and Sales, Wien-Consolidated Airlines, Alaska. He has been active in civic affairs, as well as holding many state and national posts of importance. He was president of the Alaska Chamber of Commerce, Chairman of the 1967 Alaska Centennial, and co-founder of the Annual Eskimo Olympic Games held at Fairbanks, Alaska.

LADONNA HARRIS

Mrs. Harris is the wife of U.S. Senator Fred Harris of Oklahoma, and a member of the Comanche tribe. She was active in many civic activities in the Sooner State and was voted the Outstanding American Indian Citizen in 1965. She was Chairman of the National Womans Advisory Council on the War on Poverty; Director of the Indian Peace Corps training program; and has performed many other selfless activities which have brought her people credit.

WAUHILLAU LA HAY

This Cherokee newspaper woman writes a daily column which is syndicated throughout the nation. She has been very prominent in allied areas such as public relations, radio and television. Presently, she is on the staff of the Washington Daily News and the Scripps-Howard chain.

IRA HAYES

A Pima Marine made famous as one of the men who raised the American flag at Mt. Suribachi, on Iwo Jima during World War II. Although awarded other decorations, and contrary to public opinion, he did not receive the Congressional Medal of Honor.

THOMASINE RUTH HILL

Elected "Miss Indian America XV", Miss Hill was Crow tribe princess and very active in youth work. She worked with the "Up with People" project of the Moral Re-Armament Program for several years before becoming a pre-law student at Macinac College.

LORETTA S. JENDRITZA

Major Jendritza, a Navajo, became the first woman of her tribe to attain such rank in the U.S. Air Force, and is the Operating Room Supervisor at the Air Force Academy Hospital in Colorado Springs, Colorado.

NAPOLEON B. JOHNSON

Judge Johnson, a Cherokee, became the first Chief Justice of the Supreme Court of Oklahoma of Indian ancestry. Son of a Presbyterian Elder, Judge Johnson was sent to a Presbyterian mission school and then worked his way through Tulsa University and Cumberland University, where he was awarded an L.L.B. He was a founder and served nine years as president of the National Congress of American Indians. He has received many honors.

PAUL JONES

Paul Jones served as Chairman of the Navajo Tribal Council for many years, and in doing so directed the affairs of the Navajo tribe, the largest in the nation.

BETTY MAE JUMPER

Mrs. Jumper, a Seminole from Hollywood, Florida, member of the National Council on Indian Opportunity, was the first woman in the history of her tribe to be elected tribal chairman. She and her cousin were the first Florida Seminoles to be graduated from high school. She did this over violent opposition in her family by the elders who were hostile to white men's ways. She later served as a public health nurse.

WILLIAM W. KEELER

A chief of the Cherokee nation and Executive Vice Chairman of the Board of the Phillips Petroleum Company. Considered to be the strongest tribal leader in over one hundred years, Mr. Keeler became Principal Chief in 1949. He worked his way up from the ground to his present high position of responsibility with Phillips. He has been tapped by the government to work without pay to solve problems of the industry. Along the way he has been given many honors by fraternal, veterans, civic and business groups, with whom he diligently operates. One of his initial projects was to establish the Cherokee Foundation to promote the welfare and culture of his tribe.

TED W. KEY

Overcoming the handicap of loss of parents at the early age of eleven and thereafter being raised in the Goodland Indian Orphanage, Dr. Key managed to work his way through college doing many menial jobs, and became one of the first of his race to enter dental school. His football prowess helped him earn his room, board and tuition, while barber work filled in his other needs. Later he served in the Naval Dental Corps Reserve, after two years of active duty. Dr. Key is a Choctaw Indian.

RICHARD LaCOURSE

This young Yakima-Umatilla was one of the founders of the new and vital American Indian Press Association, now headquartered in Washington, D.C., and is an active correspondent and director of its work.

MOBLEY LUSHANYA

Mrs. Lushanya made her singing debut at the Chicago City Opera. Later she went on to grand opera and a concert career in Europe. She is a Chickasaw Indian.

D'ARCY McNICKLE

This Flathead tribe member was a long-time official of the Bureau of Indian Affairs. He has done outstanding research work on the Indian and his problems. He has written and/or collaborated on many books and stories about Indians.

MARIA MARTINEZ

Known as "Maria, the Potter", this San Ildefonso Indian learned so well the skills of long-deceased artisans of clay from analysis, trial and error, and extreme patience, that she has become the most famous Indian pottery-maker. She is the only Indian woman to have been given national fame by receiving an award from the American Institute of Architects. She shapes her work free hand, with an innate sense of balance and symmetry. She was educated at Santa Fe's St. Catherine's Mission School. Her works have been placed in many museums around the country, and she has worked at most of the World's Fairs in the United States. Her gleaming, sheen-like pottery is instantly recognizable, as is her signature through the years, "Maria", "Maria and Julian", and "Maria Poveka". Her son, "Popovi-Da", has also become well known for his artistic pottery creations and lives with his mother in the pueblo. Maria has received many awards and decorations from universities, professional groups and foreign nations.

JOHN JOSEPH MATTHEWS

This Osage Indian was the first Indian to receive the coveted international Rhodes Scholarship Award. He subsequently went on to a successful writing career. Among his works are Wahkontah, Talking to the Moon, and The Osages.

RUSSELL MEANS

This Sioux Indian from the Porcupine reservation community,

South Dakota, was a leader in the many Indian activist activities of the '70s, and a moving force within AIM. He wished to turn tribal government over to the traditional Oglala forum of community representatives. He opposed Dick Wilson for tribal chairmanship in February, 1964, in which charges of fraud and harassment of voters by the U.S. Civil Rights Commission ended up in courts, where the running out of time seemed to make Means' suit meaningless.

BILLY MILLS

Born at the Pine Ridge reservation hospital on June 30, 1938, and orphaned at 13 years, he completed his first seven years of schooling at the reservation school before going on to Oglala Community School and Haskell Institute. While at Haskell, he came to public notice when he cut thirty seconds off the record of Wes Santee; for his feats the University of Kansas gave him an athletic scholarship. At that institution he became the Big Eight cross-country champion and led his team to the NCAA championship. Subsequent to graduation he joined the U.S. Marine Corps, where an officer heard about his college feats and induced Mills to resume his running efforts. After coming out on top in the service, he was sent to the Olympics where he ran against thirty-six of the most famous long-distance runners in the world. In that event he set a new Olympic record of 28:24.4 in the 10,000 meter run. Billy Mills, a Sioux Indian, is the only American ever to win a distance race in the Olympic games. The Olympic champion now resides in San Diego, California, where he is an insurance executive and takes an active role in youth activities, including Boy Scout leadership programs.

N. SCOTT MOMADAY

An associate professor of English at the University of California, this Kiowa Indian won the coveted Pulitzer Prize for Literature, for his book House Made Of Dawn, and thereby became the first member of his race to be so honored. The son of famous artists, Mr. and Mrs. Al Momaday, of Jemez Pueblo, who are also educators, he grew up and lived on many reservations. He received a bachelor's degree from the University of New Mexico in 1958 and then taught at the Dulce, N.M. Jicarilla Apache reservation before entering Stanford in 1960, where he subsequently received his M.A. and Ph. D. He is also the author of The Way to Rainy Mountain, a collection of Kiowa legends. Momaday was a Stanford Creative Writing Fellow in poetry in 1959-60 and a Guggenheim Fellow in 1966-67. He resides with his wife and two children in Goleta, California.

NATACHEE SCOTT MOMADAY

Mrs. Momaday, a Cherokee-Choctaw, is the wife of Al Momaday, noted teacher/artist of Jemez Pueblo, New Mexico, and the mother of teacher/author N. Scott Momaday. Educated at Haskell Institute and a graduate of the University of California at Los Angeles where she received a B.A. degree. Her writings have included over fifty articles, and the books American Indian Authors (Houghton-Mifflin 1972) and Owl in the Cedar Tree (Ginn, 1965, republished by Northland Press 1975).

DOMINGO MONTOYA

This Sandia Pueblo Indian is the Chairman of the All-Indian Pueblo Council in New Mexico, and is the only governor of the pueblo to hold the position for two consecutive years. He has also represented his pueblo and state on many national and international committees and commissions.

MAJOR GENERAL LLOYD R. MOSES

Born in Fairfax, South Dakota, September 30, 1904, on the Sioux Indian reservation, he attended the University of South Dakota from 1927 to 1931. After graduation he took graduate work and taught chemistry at Sioux Falls College. General Moses, a Rosebud Sioux Indian, served in the European theatre of operations during World War II and in Korea where he was at one time the Senior United Nations Commander. Subsequently, he was advanced in rank and was Deputy Commanding General of the 5th Army when he retired in 1961. During his service he conducted private studies on educational problems in the U.S. Army. Recently he has been connected with the work of the Office of Economic Affairs in Vermillion, South Dakota. For his work in the service he has received many decorations, including the Distinguished Service Cross and the Silver Star.

JOHNSTON MURRAY

Johnston Murray, a Chickasaw, became the fourteenth Governor of the State of Oklahoma.

RAMOND NAKAI

Mr. Nakai has been the paid, full-time Chairman of the Navajo Tribal Council for a number of years. In that time the Navajos have shown remarkable changes in their economic status and educational attainments.

JAMES C. OTTIPOBY

Reverend Ottipoby, a Comanche Indian, was the first of his tribe to be awarded a college degree, and later, during World War II, became the first Indian commissioned in the Army Chaplain Corps. Emerging from the typical wandering life of his people, he subsequently went to reservation and public schools. Later, he was awarded a B.A. from Hope College and his theological degree from Western Seminary. He has served Presbyterian churches on the Winnebago reservation, at Laguna Pueblo and in Albuquerque, N.M.

MARIA TALLCHIEF PASCHEN

Maria Tallchief Paschen (Osage) has made her mark in the world of dancing and became one of the leading ballerinas. She made her debut in classical ballet at the age of fifteen years in the Hollywood Bowl, after studying from three years of age. She joined the Ballet Russe de Monte Carlo in 1942 at the age of eighteen. In 1947 she was guest star with the Paris Opera Company, and from 1947 to 1960 she was with the New York City Ballet, becoming their Premiere Ballerina in 1954, a remarkable feat for one of less than thirty years of age. In 1960 she switched to the American Ballet Theatre (now the New York City Ballet Company). Her sister, Marjorie Skibine, dances with the Paris Opera Ballet.

FRANK PERATROVICH

This Thlingit tribe Alaskan lawmaker has served in the Territorial and State legislatures since 1944, during which time he has held many posts, including President of the Senate.

EARL OLD PERSON

This 40-year old member of the Blackfeet Tribe of Montana is Chairman of his Tribal Council, President of Affiliated Tribes of the Northwest Indians, and a member of the Educational Advisory Board for Montana State University. He has been active in Indian dances and ceremonials, and has worked closely with Boy Scouts, 4-H Clubs, Lions Clubs, the Jaycees, and many other organizations. He is engaged in ranching in Browning, Montana. On October 10, 1969, he was elected president of the National Congress of American Indians.

DILLON PLATERO

This young Navajo founded and was the first editor of the Navajo Times, tribal newspaper for that nation. He has been very active in Indian education.

JOHN C. RANIER

This Taos Indian is the present Executive Director of the New Mexico Commission on Indian Affairs. On October 10, 1969, he was elected the first vice-president of the National Congress of American Indians. He is a rancher and operator of a mercantile store at Taos Pueblo. A product of schooling at Santa Fe Indian School and Bacone Junior College, he holds a B.A. Degree in education and a Master's Degree from the University of Southern California. He was the Executive Secretary of the National Congress of American Indians, Chairman of the All-Indian Pueblo Council, a member of the Board of Directors for the American Indian Development, Inc., Director of the Ute Rehabilitation Program, Ute Mountain Agency, a teacher at Indian schools and principal of the Taos Day School.

BEN REIFEL

This Sioux Indian is a U.S. Congressman from South Dakota who received undergraduate training at South Dakota State University, and an M.A. and Ph.D. from Harvard. His early vocational endeavors included serving his home reservation as farm agent and an eventual return as the first Indian superintendent. He saw service in the European theatre during World War II and holds a rank of Lt. Colonel in the Reserves. He studied under a faculty scholarship and was honored with a John Hay Whitney Fellowship award. Coming from a family where his mother spoke little English, he and his brother Alexander, a civil engineer, and Albert, a doctor specializing in internal medicine with the U.S. Veterans Administration, form a family worthy of emulation by anyone, for they worked their way into positions in American society where they are indeed in the "mainstream" and participating in all of its benefits.

WILL ROGERS, JR.

Will Rogers, Jr., a Cherokee Indian, was elected to the 78th U.S. Congress from California from January 1943 until May 1944. He is an actor, humorist and newspaper publisher as well as a member of the California legislature at other times. He served in World War II as 2nd Lt. AUS. He received a B.A. from Stanford Univ. He is presently Special Assistant to the Commissioner of Indian Affairs.

JOE SANDO

This Jemez Pueblo (New Mexico) Indian is the Director of the All-Pueblo Indian Education Project Talent Search. He received a B.A. from New Mexico University and an M.A. from Vanderbilt University. He has written in the field of audiology which was his field of concentration for his advanced degree. He is a World War II Navy veteran. Active in many civic and state affairs which concern the Indian, he is the author of numerous articles on Indian problems and history.

BUFFY SAINTE-MARIE

Born in 1942 of undetermined Cree Indian parents and later adopted early in childhood by a Micmac couple, this folksinger and composer was reared in Wakefield, Mass. She was a shy and lonely child, who taught herself to play the guitar. She was an honor student at the University of Massachusetts where she received her degree. After graduation she moved to New York where she perfected a low, throaty singing style which "caught on" along with her self-composed folksongs. She has become a "big time" entertainer, although claiming not to be a "protest singer." She definitely if of the "young breed" of youthful Indians who are not content to sit idly, while the world marches by.

MARTIN SENECA

He was born and reared on the Seneca Indian reservation in western New York state. He is married, the father of three children, and thirty-three years of age. Mr. Seneca received B.S. and M.S. degrees from Brigham Young University and a J.D. from Harvard Law School. He served as a White House Fellow, 1971-72.

KEN SISSONS

A Rosebud Sioux Indian who fought in World War II, he is probably the most decorated soldier in South Dakota.

ALONZO SPANG

Mr. Spang, a Northern Cheyenne, is the Vice-President of the Navajo Community College at Many Farms, Arizona, and was formerly the President of the Cook Christian College in Tempe, Arizona. Although he was prematurely identified as Indian Commissioner by the Secretary of the Interior during the summer of 1969, his appointment was not confirmed by the President.

MORRIS THOMPSON

This Athabascan Indian, born in Tanawa, Alaska, started in the public school there and attended the University of Alaska where he majored in Civil Engineering and completed college work in California. After a number of years in private industry, he transferred his interest into government and subsequently held various positions with the Bureau of Indian Affairs, culminating with his appointment as Commissioner on December 3, 1973. A Republican, he is considered to have a promising future in Alaskan politics, although he professes to have no plans to announce for public office.

PABLITA VELARDE

Generally acknowledged to be the foremost Indian woman artist, "Golden Dawn" has been able to gain the attention and respect of the entire art world for art works which show tremendous quantities of precise and finite details. Professing to having been sightless at one time and subsequently having taught herself to remember and absorb the smallest details of things and persons, Pablita, a Santa Clara Pueblo Indian, never found a need for a model or photo. She is noted for her work in earth colors and has taught at the Santa Fe Indian School. Her beautiful and talented daughter, Helen Harden, follows in her mother's footsteps, but has an individual approach and philosophy concerning her art.

WILMA L. VICTOR

This fifty-five year old member of the Choctaw Tribe, Oklahoma, was appointed special assistant for Indian Affairs in the Interior Department in 1971, after a long career in the federal service and the first woman to hold such a high position at the secretarial level, and only the second person as an assistant to the Secretary for Indian Affairs. She was former principal of the Institute of American Arts in Santa Fe, New Mexico, and the Intermountain School, in Utah.

ANNIE DODGE WAUNEKA

Daughter of the famed Navajo Chief, Chee Dodge, this tireless woman was the first Indian woman given the Presidential Medal of Freedom Award. The citation accompanying it tells only a minute part of her life story: "First woman elected to the Navajo Tribal Council; by her long crusade for improved health programs, she has helped dramatically to lessen the menace of disease among her people and to improve their way of life." She was honored by CBS television commentator Walter Cronkite, who devoted one of his world-famous 20th Century documentary films to her work in education, health and better living for the Navajos, despite years of opposition from those who were tradition-minded in their approaches to living in the fast-changing world about them. Her philosophy was summed up in one of her oft-quoted remarks to her people: "Send your children to school. Learn the new ways. What is good for the white man's children is good for ours. Prejudice and tradition must be overcome."

GERALD T. WILKINSON

This Cherokee-Catawba Indian has been the executive director of the National Indian Youth Council since 1968 and a vital force in focusing public attention on the problems of the Indian youths.

DR. EVELYN YELLOW ROBE

Dr. Evelyn Yellow Robe of the Rosebud Sioux Reservation attended

Mt. Holyoke College, Northwestern University and Vassar College (certainly some of the most demanding colleges of America) and was honored by a Fulbright Scholarship. She has taught at Vassar College and is now on the staff of Northwestern University Medical School where she is engaged in research and teaching in audiology and voice disorders. While at Vassar she spent a summer in South Dakota on the Pine Ridge and Rosebud reservations, recording the Dakota language.

POPULATION

The question, "Who is an Indian?" can be answered in a variety of ways. There are "administrative", "official", and census -- sometimes called "cultural" -- definitions; however, for general use, Indians might be defined as "those who are members of tribes with Federal trust land, who have one-quarter Indian blood and who live on a Federal reservation, or nearby." The tables herewith do not include all Indians in the country, and estimates as to their variance range as high as 200,000.

United States Census Enumerations of Indians: 1890-1960[1]
for the United States excluding Alaska

Year	Total Enumerated	Adjusted for Underenumeration[2]	Alaskan Natives
1890	248,300		25,400
1900	237,200		29,500
1910	265,700		25,300
1920	244,400		26,600
1930	332,400		30,000
1940	334,000	360,500	32,500
1950	342,400	421,600	33,900
1960	509,100	2	43,100
1965 (est.)	555,000[3]		45,000[3]
1970 (est.)	600,000[4]		47,500[4]
1970 (act.)	760,600		50,600
1973 (est.)	791,800		

1. United States Bureau of the Census, Decennial Census Publications; all figures rounded to the nearest hundred.

2. Adjustments were made for underenumeration in 1940 and 1950. In these censuses, due to the enumeration procedures used, many Indians of mixed racial background were not identified as Indians. The self-enumeration procedures used in the 1960 Census resulted in a larger proportion of such persons being returned as Indians.

3. Public Health Service, Division of Indian Health current mid-decade estimate based on post censal year projections.

4. Author's projection based upon study of birth/death statistics. There are a large number of relatively static populations, sometimes due to migration. Other groups, notably in the Southwest, are experiencing a quite rapid increase. This is especially true where the Navajos seem to be revealing a 3 percent annual increase.

INDIAN WARS AND LOCAL DISTURBANCES

1782-1787 --   Wyoming Valley war in Pennsylvania.

1790-1795 --   War with the Northwest Indians; Mingo, Miami, Wyandot,
               Delaware, Potawatomi, Shawnee, Chippewa, and Ottawa,
               September 19, 1790 to August 3, 1795.

1811 --   War with the Indians, September 21 to November 18.

1812 --   Florida or Seminole war, August 15 to October.

1813 --   Peoria Indian war in Illinois, September 19 to October 21.

1813-1814 --   Creek Indian war in Alabama, Georgia, Mississippi, and
               Tennessee, July 27, 1813 to August 9, 1814.

1817-1818 --   Seminole Indian war in Georgia and Florida, November 20,
               1817 to October 31, 1818.

1823 --   Campaign against Arickaree Indians, upper Missouri River.

1827 --   Fever River expedition against the Indians in Illinois.

1827 --   Winnebago expedition, Wisconsin, June 28 to September 27,
               1827; also called La Fevre Indian war.

1831 --   Sac and Fox Indian war in Illinois, June and July.

1832 --   Black Hawk Indian war, April 26 to September 30, 1832, in
               Illinois and Wisconsin.

1834 --   Pawnee expedition in the Indian Territory, June to September.

1835-1836 --   The Toledo war, or Ohio and Michigan boundary dispute.

1835-1842 --   Florida or Seminole Indian war in Florida, Georgia, and
               Alabama, December 8, 1835 to August 14, 1842.

1836-1837 --   Sabine or Southwestern Indian disturbance in Louisiana,
               April, 1836 to April, 1837.

1836-1837 --   Creek disturbance in Alabama, May 5, 1836 to September
               30, 1837.

INDIAN WARS AND LOCAL DISTURBANCES (continued)

1836 --   Heatherly Indian troubles on Missouri and Iowa line, July
               to November.

1836-1838 --   Cherokee disturbances and removal to the Indian Territory.

1837 --   Osage Indian war in Missouri.

1847-1848 --   Cayuse Indian war in Oregon, December, 1847 to July, 1848.

1849-1855 --   Texas and New Mexico Indian war.

1849-1855 --   Apache, Navajo, and Utah war.

1849-1861 --   Navajo troubles in New Mexico.

1849-1861 --   Continuous disturbances with Comanche, Cyenenne, Lipan,
               and Kickapoo Indians in Texas.

1850 --   Pit River expedition, California, April 28 to September 13.

1850-1853 --   Utah Indian disturbances.

1851-1852 --   California Indian disturbances.

1851-1856 --   Rogue River Indian war in Oregon; June 17 to July 3, 1851;
               August 8 to September, 1853; March to June, 1856.

1854 --   Oregon Indian war in Oregon, August and September, 1854.

1855 --   Yakima expedition, Washington Territory, October 11 to
               November 24.

1855 --   Klamath and Salmon River Indian war in Oregon and Idaho,
               January to March.

1855 --   Winna's expedition against Snake Indians, Oregon, May 24
               to September 8.

1855-1856 --   Sioux expedition, Nebraska Territory, April 3, 1855 to
               July 27, 1856.

1855-1856 --   Cheyenne and Arapaho troubles.

1855-1858 --   Florida Indian war, December 15, 1855 to May 8, 1858.

1857 --   Sioux Indian troubles in Minnesota and Iowa, March and
               April, 1857.

INDIAN WARS AND LOCAL DISTURBANCES (continued)

1858 --   Expedition against northern Indians, Washington Territory,
                 July 17 to October 17.

1858 --   Spokane, Coeur d'Alene, and Paloos Indian troubles.

1858 --   Navajo expedition, New Mexico, September 9 to December 25.

1858-1859 --   Wichita expedition, Indian Territory, September 11, 1858
                 to December, 1859.

1859 --   Colorado River expedition, California, February 11 to
                 April 28.

1859 --   Pecos expedition, Texas, April 16 to August 17.

1860 --   Kiowa and Comanche expedition, Indian Territory, May 8
                 to October 11.

1860-1861 --   Navajo expedition, New Mexico, September 12, 1860 to
                 February 24, 1861.

1861-1864 --   Campaign against the Cheyenne Indians.

1862-1863 --   Sioux Indian war in Minnesota and Dakota. In 1863 the Minne-
                 sota Sioux were removed to Dakota.

1863-1869 --   War against the Cheyenne, Arapaho, Kiowa, and Comanche
                 Indians in Kansas, Nebraska, Colorado, and Indian Territory.

1865-1868 --   Campaign against Indians in southern Oregon, Idaho, and
                 northern California.

1867-1869 --   Campaign against Indians in Kansas, Colorado, and Indian
                 Territory.

1867-1881 --   Campaign against Lipan, Kickapoo, and Comanche Indians,
                 and Mexican border disturbances.

1872-1873 --   Modoc Indian war in Oregon and California, November 22,
                 1872 to October 3, 1873.

1873 --   Campaign against Apache Indians in Arizona and New Mexico.

1874 --   Sioux expedition, Wyoming and Nebraska, February 13 to
                 August.

INDIAN WARS AND LOCAL DISTURBANCES (continued)

1872-1873 --   Modoc Indian war in Oregon and California, November 22, 1872 to October 3, 1873.

1873 --   Campaign against Apache Indians in Arizona and New Mexico.

1874-1875 --   Campaign against Kiowa, Cheyenne, and Comanche Indians in Indian Territory, August 1, 1874 to February 16, 1875.

1875 --   Expedition against Indians in eastern Nevada, September 7 to 27.

1876-1877 --   Big Horn and Yellowstone expeditions, Wyoming and Montana, February 17, 1876 to June 13, 1877.

1876-1879 --   War with Northern Cheyenne Indians in Indian Territory, Kansas, Wyoming, Dakota, Nebraska, and Montana.

1877 --   Nez Perce Indian war in Utah, May 14 to October 1.

1878 --   Bannock Indian war in Idaho, Washington Territory, and Wyoming Territory.

1878-1879 --   Campaign against Cheyenne Indians in Dakota and Montana.

1879 --   Ute expedition, Colorado, April 3 to September 9.

1879 --   Snake or Sheepeater Indian troubles, Idaho, August to October.

1879 --   White River campaign against Ute Indians in Utah and Colorado, September 29, to October 5.

1890-1891 --   Sioux Indian disturbances in South Dakota, November, 1890 to January, 1891.

1898 --   Chippewa Indian disturbances, Leech Lake, October.

U.S. ADMINISTRATORS OF FEDERAL INDIAN POLICY

Secretaries of War (1789 to 1832)	Year of Appointment	President
Henry Knox[1]	1789	George Washington
Thomas Pickering	1795	George Washington
James McHenry	1796	George Washington and John Adams
Samuel Dexter	1800	John Adams
Henry Dearborn	1801	Thomas Jefferson
William Eustis	1809	James Madison
John Armstrong	1813	James Madison
James Monroe	1814	James Madison
William H. Crawford	1815	James Madison and James Monroe
John C. Calhoun[2]	1817	James Monroe
James Barbour[2]	1825	John Quincy Adams
Peter B. Porter[2]	1828	John Quincy Adams
John H. Eaton[2]	1829	Andrew Jackson
Lewis Cass[2]	1831	Andrew Jackson

Commissioners of Indian Affairs (1832 to Present)		
Elbert Herring	1832	Andrew Jackson
Carey A. Harris	1836	Andrew Jackson and Martin Van Buren
T. Hartley Crawford	1838	Martin Van Buren, William H. Harrison and John Tyler

[1] Knox served as "Secretary in the War Office" from 1784. Prior to that, from 1775 on, Indian affairs had been carried on by Indian Commissioners from three departments, responsible to the Continental Congress.

[2] On March 11, 1824, John Calhoun named Thomas L. McKenny, who had served from 1816-22 as Superintendent of Indian Trade under the War Department, to be the "head" of the Bureau of Indian Affairs within the War Department. McKenny served in this capacity under Secretaries Calhoun, Barbour, Porter, and Eaton, until replaced by Samuel S. Hamilton on September 30, 1831. Hamilton was in turn succeeded by Elbert Herring in 1831, who a year later became the first Commissioner of Indian Affairs by an Act of Congress.

U.S. ADMINISTRATORS OF FEDERAL INDIAN POLICY (continued)

Commissioners of Indian Affairs (1832 to Present)	Year of Appointment	President
William Medill	1845	James K. Polk and Zachary Taylor
Orlando Brown	1849	Zachary Taylor and Millard Fillmore
Luke Lea	1850	Millard Fillmore
George Manypenny	1853	Franklin Pierce
James W. Denver	1857	James Buchanan
Charles E. Mix	1858	James Buchanan
James W. Denver	1858	James Buchanan
Alfred B. Greenwood	1859	James Buchanan
William P. Dole	1861	Abraham Lincoln and Andrew Johnson
Dennis Cooley	1865	Andrew Johnson
Lewis V. Bogy	1866	Andrew Johnson
Nathaniel G. Taylor	1867	Andrew Johnson
Eli S. Parker	1869	Ulysses S. Grant
Francis A. Walker	1871	Ulysses S. Grant
Edward P. Smith	1873	Ulysses S. Grant
John O. Smith	1875	Ulysses S. Grant and R. B. Hayes
Ezra A. Hayt	1877	Rutherford B. Hayes
R. E. Trowbridge	1880	Rutherford B. Hayes
Hiram Price	1881	James Garfield and Chester A. Arthur
John D. C. Atkins	1885	Grover Cleveland
John H. Oberly	1888	Grover Cleveland
Thomas J. Morgan	1889	Benjamin Harrison
Daniel M. Browning	1893	Grover Cleveland
William A. Jones	1897	William McKinley and Theodore Roosevelt
Francis E. Leupp	1904	Theodore Roosevelt
Robert G. Valentine	1909	William Howard Taft
Cato Sells	1913	Woodrow Wilson
Charles H. Burke	1921	Warren G. Harding and and Calvin Coolidge
Charles J. Rhoads	1929	Herbert Hoover
John Collier	1933	Franklin D. Roosevelt
William A. Brophy	1945	Franklin D. Roosevelt and Harry S Truman
John R. Nichols	1949	Harry S Truman

U.S. ADMINISTRATORS OF FEDERAL INDIAN POLICY (continued)

Commissioners of Indian Affairs (1832 to Present)	Year of Appointment	President
Dillon S. Myer	1950	Harry S Truman
Glenn L. Emmons	1953	Dwight D. Eisenhower
Philleo Nash	1961	John F. Kennedy and Lyndon B. Johnson
Robert L. Bennett	1966	Lyndon B. Johnson
Louis R. Bruce	1969	Richard M. Nixon
Vacant	Dec. 8, 1972 to Dec. 3, 1973	
Morris Thompson	1973	Richard M. Nixon

GOVERNMENT APPROPRIATIONS FOR INDIAN EDUCATION

Year	Appropriation	Year	Appropriation
1877	$ 20,000	1900	$2,936,080
1878	30,000	1901	3,080,367
1879	60,000	1902	3,244,250
1880	75,000	1903	3,531,250
1881	75,000	1904	3,522,950
1882	135,000	1905	3,880,740
1883	487,000	1906	3,777,100
1884	675,200	1907	3,925,830
1885	992,800	1908	4,105,715
1886	1,110,065	1909	4,008,825
1887	1,211,415	1910	3,757,909
1888	1,179,916	1911	3,685,290
1889	1,348,015	1912	3,757,495
1890	1,364,568	1913	4,015,720
1891	1,842,770	1914	4,403,355
1892	2,291,650	1915	4,678,627
1893	2,315,612	1916	4,391,155
1894	2,243,497	1917	4,701,903
1895	2,060,695	1918	5,185,290
1896	2,056,515	1919	4,835,300
1897	2,517,265	1920	4,922,325
1898	2,631,771	1921	4,725,825
1899	2,638,390		

GOVERNMENT APPROPRIATIONS FOR INDIAN EDUCATION (continued)

Year	Appropriation	Year	Appropriation
1929	$ 2,565,000	1957	$42,620,000
1930	2,850,000	1958	46,536,000
1940	6,034,790	1959	47,987,000
1947	11,139,700	1960	47,432,000
1948	11,139,700	1961	51,653,000
1949	11,176,000	1962	54,332,000
1950	13,207,000	1963	63,420,000
1951	21,838,722	1964	66,109,000
1952	24,301,197	1965	70,099,000
1953	26,173,410	1966	76,074,000
1954	26,227,000	1967	84,400,000
1955	32,951,647	1968	88,199,000
1956	38,409,395	1969	95,459,000

Source, 1877-1921: U.S. Department of the Interior. Report of the
Commissioner of Indian Affairs for the fiscal year
ended June 30, 1920.

Source, 1929-1969: U.S. Budget; Bureau of Indian Affairs

INDIAN MUSEUMS

(A short selection of some of the more
well-known museums and art collections.)

Anadarko City Museum
Anadarko, Oklahoma 73005

American Museum of Natural History
New York, N.Y. 10024

Brooklyn Museum
Brooklyn, N.Y. 11213

Bureau of American Ethnology
The Smithsonian Institute
Washington, D.C. 20560

Bureau of Indian Affairs
Washington, D.C. 20242

Carnegie Institution of Washington
Washington, D.C. 20565

Carnegie Museum
Pittsburgh, Pennsylvania

Chicago Natural History Museum
Chicago, Ill. 60605

Denver Art Museum
Chappell House
Denver, Colorado 80203

Field Museum of Natural History
Chicago, Ill. 60605

Harvard University
Peabody Museum of Archaeology and
   Ethnology
Cambridge, Mass. 02100

Heard Museum of Anthropology and
   Primative Art
Phoenix, Arizona 85000

Sheldon Jackson Museum
Sitka, Alaska

Frank H. McClung Museum
Knoxville, Tennessee

Milwaukee Public Museum
Milwaukee, Wisconsin

Museum of the American Indian
Heye Foundation
New York, N.Y. 10000

Museum of the Cherokee Indian
Cherokee, North Carolina 28719

Museum of Indian Art
San Francisco, California 94131

Museum of Navajo Ceremonial Art
Santa Fe, New Mexico 87501

Museum of New Mexico
Hall of Ethnology of the Laboratory
   of Anthropology
Santa Fe, New Mexico 87501

Museum of Northern Arizona
Flagstaff, Arizona 86001

Museum of the Plains Indians
   and Crafts Center
Browning, Montana 59417

Museum of Primative Art
New York, N.Y. 10019

Navajo Tribal Museum
Window Rock, Arizona 86515

INDIAN MUSEUMS (continued)

The New York State Museum
Albany, New York

Osage Tribal Museum
Pawhuska, Oklahoma 74056

Panhandle Plains Historical Museum
Amarillo, Texas

Philbrook Art Center
Tulsa, Oklahoma 74114

Pipestone National Monument
Pipestone, Minnesota 56164

Rochester Museum of Arts and Sciences
Rochester, New York 14600

San Diego Museum of Man
San Diego, California 92100

School of American Research
Santa Fe, N.M. 87501

Sioux Indian Museum and Crafts Center
Rapid City, S.D. 57701

Southeast Museum of the North
   American Indian
Marathon, Florida 33050

Southern Plains Indian Museum and
   Crafts Center
Anadarko, Oklahoma 73005

Southwest Museum
Los Angeles, California 90000

The Thomas Gilcrease Institute of
   American History and Art
Tulsa, Oklahoma 74101

University of Alaska Museum
College, Alaska 99735

University of Arizona
Arizona State Museum
Tucson, Arizona 85700

University of California
Robert H. Lowie Museum of
   Anthropology
Berkley, California 94700

University of Kentucky
Museum of Anthropology
Lexington, Kentucky 40500

University of Michigan
Museum of Anthropology
Ann Arbor, Michigan 48103

University of Missouri
Museum of Anthropology
Columbia, Missouri 65201

University of Oklahoma
Library
Norman, Oklahoma 70369

University of Pennsylvania
University Museum
Philadelphia, Pennsylvania 19100

University of Utah
Anthropology Museum
Salt Lake City, Utah 84100

University of Washington
Thomas Burke Memorial
Washington State Museum
Seattle, Washington 98100

Wayne State University
Museum of Anthropology
Detroit, Michigan 48200

Whitney Museum of Modern Art
New York, N. Y.

Wisconsin State Historical Society
Madison, Wisconsin

A FEW INDIAN GROUPS

American Indian Historical Society
1451 Masonic Avenue
San Francisco, California 94117

Membership $10.00 per year which includes a subscription
to The Indian Historian. Maintains an Indian Library and
archives. Research scholars should apply for special research privileges. Tours and talks arranged.

Arrow, Inc.
1346 Connecticut Avenue, N.W.
Washington, D.C. 20036

 Association on American Indian Affairs
432 Park Avenue, South
New York, N.Y. 10016
(non-Indian group)

Indian Rights Association, Inc.
1505 Race Street
Philadelphia, Penn.
(non-Indian group since 1885)

National Congress of American Indians
1346 Connecticut Avenue, N.W.
Washington, D.C. 20036

National American Indian Movement (AIM)
Box 3677
St. Paul, Minnesota 55101

National Indian Youth Council
Formed in 1961 -- activist group
Various offices, including:

> Box 3175
> East Colfax Street
> Denver, Colorado 80218

> One Garden Circle
> Hotel Claremont
> Berkley, California 94705

> 3102 Central Avenue, S.E.
> Albuquerque, New Mexico 87107

Native American Elders United
808 Ivy Street
Carson City, Nevada

SOME INDIAN PUBLICATIONS

ABC -- American Before Columbus
National Indian Youth Council
Box 3175, East Colfax Street
Denver, Colorado 80218

Akwesasne Notes

Mohawk Nation
Via Rooseveltown, N.Y. 13683

American Indian Culture Center Journal

University of California
Room 3221, Campbell Hall
405 Hilgard Avenue
Los Angeles, California 90024

American Indian Law Newsletter
University of New Mexico
School of Law
1915 Roma Avenue, N.E.
Albuquerque, N.M. 87106

American Indian News

Thunderbird American Indian Dancers
M.D. Meixner
5 Tudor Place
New York, N.Y. 10017

The Amerindian
(American Indian Review)
Marion E. Gridely, Ed.
1263 W. Pratt Boulevard
Chicago, Illinois 60626

The Cherokee One Feather

Eastern Band of Cherokee Indians
P.O. Box 501
Cherokee, N.C. 28719

The Cherokee Times
Box 105
Cherokee, N.C. 28719

City Smoke Signals
Sioux City American Indian Center
1114 West 6th Street
Sioux City, Iowa

Education Journal

Institute for the Development of Indian Law
927 - 15th St., N.W., Suite 612
Washington, D.C. 20005

Ethnohistory
American Society for Ethnohistory
State University of New York
205 Foster Hall
Buffalo, New York

Fort Apache Scout
White Apache Tribal Council
P.O. Box 898
Whiteriver, Arizona 85941

Indian Affairs
Association on American Indian Affairs
432 Park Avenue, South
New York, N.Y. 10016

The Indian Historian
1451 Masonic Avenue
San Francisco, California 94117

The Indian Leader
Haskell Institute
Lawrence, Kansas

The Indian Newsletter
Access -- Indian Project
Box 106
Pala, California 92059

SOME INDIAN PUBLICATIONS (continued)

Indian Record
Bureau of Indian Affairs
Department of the Interior
1951 Constitution Avenue, N.W.
Washington, D.C. 20242

The Indian Reporter
3254 Orange Street
Riverside, Calif. 92501

Indian Truth
Indian Rights Association, Inc.
1505 Race Street
Philadelphia, Penn.

Indian Voices
Robert K. Thuma, Ed.
University of Chicago
1126 East 59th Street
Chicago, Illinois 60637

Journal of American Indian Education
Arizona State University
Tempe, Arizona 85281

Maine Indian Newsletter
Eugenia T. Thompson, Ed.
42 Liberty Street
Gardiner, Maine 04345

Many Smokes
Sun Bear, Editor
P.O. Box 5895
Reno, Nevada 89503

The Native Nevadan
Inter-tribal Council of Nevada, Inc.
1995 East 2nd Street
Reno, Nevada 89502

Navajo Times
Navajo Tribal Council
Box 428
Window Rock, Arizona 86515

Papago Indian News
Sells, Arizona

Rosebud Sioux Herald (Eyapaha)
Rosebud Sioux Tribal Council
Rosebud, South Dakota

The Sentinal
Official Publication
National Congress of American Indians
1346 Connecticut Avenue, N.W.
Washington, D.C.

The Smoke Signal
Federated Indians of California
2727 Santa Clara Way
Sacramento, California 95817

Smoke Signals
Colorado River Indian Tribes
Parker, Arizona 85344

Tundra Times
Eskimo-Indian-Aleut Newspaper
Fairbanks, Alaska

U.S. Indian Educational Newsletter
U.S. Office of Education
Office of Programs for Disadvantaged
400 Maryland Avenue, S.W.
Washington, D.C. 20202

The Voice of the Brotherhood
P.O. Box 1418
Juneau, Alaska

The Warrior
American Indian Center
4605 N. Pauline Street
Chicago, Ill. 60640

Wassaja
A Native Newspaper of Indian America
American Indian Historical Society
1451 Masonic Avenue
San Francisco, Calif. 94117

A FEW AUDIO-VISUAL SUGGESTIONS

In addition to the few films and film strips cited, the reader is referred to the usual distributors and trade sources, as well as to University film libraries which exist in veritably every state.

FILMS

The American Indian Influence on the
   United States

Dana Productions
6249 Babcock Avenue
North Hollywood, Ca. 91606

Best of Two Worlds
Bureau of Sport Fisheries and Wildlife
Fish and Wildlife Service
U.S. Department of the Interior
Washington, D.C.

Children of the Plains Indians (P,I,J)*
McGraw-Hill Book Company
Text Film Department
330 West 42nd Street
New York, N.Y. 10036

Eye of the Heart
Sid Darion, Manager of Public Affairs
ABC News
7 West 66th Street
New York, N.Y. 10023

Indian Artists of the Southwest (M-J)
EBE Films

Indian Boy of the Southwest
Film Associates
11559 Santa Monica Blvd.
Los Angeles, California

Indians on Parade (P,I,J,S,A)*
New Mexico Department of
   Development
302 Galisteo Street
Santa Fe, New Mexico 87501

Native American Arts
Indian Arts and Crafts Board
Bureau of the Interior
Free Loan available through:
Modern Talking Pictures
2323 New Hyde Park Road
New Hyde Park, N.Y. 11040

Pueblo Indians of the Southwest
McGraw-Hill Book Company
Text Film Division
330 West 42nd Street
New York, N.Y. 10036

Spirit of the White Mountains (S,A)*
Avalon Daggett Productions
P.O. Box 14656
Baton Rouge, Louisiana 70800

The Forgotten American
(CBS News Special)
Carousel Films, Inc.
1501 Broadway
New York, N.Y. 10012

Washoe
Western Artists Corporation
2790 Sycamore Canyon Road
Santa Barbara, California 93103

Some films available from the usual state loan or university rental libraries:
American Indians as Seen by D. H. Lawrence
Navajo Night Dances
Painting with Sand

National Park Service Films. Write to Regional Office. Free Rentals.
The Carvings of a Canyon, Grand Canyon National Park
Shadow of the Buffalo, Yellowstone National Park
The Silent City, Mesa Verde National Park

*P - Primary Grade Groups   S - Senior High School
 I - Intermediate Grade Groups   A - Adult
 J - Junior High School

AUDIO-VISUAL SUGGESTIONS (continued)

FILM STRIPS

American Indian

McGraw-Hill
New York, N.Y. 10036

The American Indian: A Study in Depth

Schloat Productions, Inc.
150 White Plains Road
Tarrytown, N.Y. 10591

The First Americans: Cultural Patterns

Schloat Productions, Inc.
150 White Plains Road
Tarrytown, N.Y. 10591

Chief Pontiac
In Westward Expansion Series 11350
Encyclopedia Brittanica Educational
    Corporation

Indian Cultures of the Americas
In American Heritage Series 10630
Encyclopedia Britannica Educational
    Corporation

Indians of North America

National Geographic Society
Washington, D.C. 20036

Minorities Have Made America Great
Part Two, "American Indians Parts I & II"
written by Barbara Martinsons and
    Sherwin S. Glassner
produced by Warren Schloat Productions,
Inc., 1968
Pleasantville, New York 10570

RECORDS

Apache Songs
Archive of Folk Song
The Library of Congress
Washington, D.C. 20540

Indian Music of the Southwest
Ethnic Folkways Library
Folkways Records & Service Corp
117 West 46th Street
New York, N.Y.

Indian Songs of Today
Archive of Folk Song
The Library of Congress
Washington, D.C. 20540

Music of the American Indians of
    the Southwest
Ethnic Folkways Library
Folkways Records & Service Corp.
117 West 46th Street
New York, N.Y.

OTHERS

Indians of New Mexico, a large
    wall-size map
Hearne Brothers, Detroit, Michigan

The Plight of the American Indians
Current Affairs Filmstrips No. 306
Key Productions, Inc.
527 Madison Avenue
New York, N.Y. 10022

The American Indian
Warren Schloat Productions, Inc.
Pleasantville, New York 10570

White Man and Indian: The First Contacts
Multi-Media Productions
Stanford, California 94305

Music of Sioux and Navajo
Ethnic Folkways Library
Folkways Records & Service Corp.
117 West 46th Street
New York, N.Y.

North American Indian Songs
Children's Music Center, Inc.
5373 Peso Blvd.
Los Angeles, Calif.

Pueblo Music: Taos, San Ildefonso,
    Zuni and Hopi
Archive of Folk Song
The Library of Congress
Washington, D.C. 20540

7 More Taos Indian Songs
Taos Recordings and Publications
P. O. Box 246
Taos, New Mexico

A READING AND RESEARCH BIBLIOGRAPHY

Note: The reader is cautioned to avoid jumping to the hasty conclusion that the following is given as a comprehensive bibliography; it is, in reality, merely what the title above states: *A Bibliography*. The interested person will find much of interest in such governmental sources as The Bureau of Indian Affairs publications and reports; the Office of Anthropology, Smithsonian Institute; the National Archives and Records Service; and the U.S. Government Printing Office. Many states offer free or inexpensive material bearing upon Indians. Colleges and universities, and their presses, have issued many outstanding publications. (Particularly outstanding is the University of Oklahoma Press, as well as those located in states with high densities of Indian population — present or past.)

In substance, then, armed with the above knowledge and the bibliography about to be presented, the interested party may start to read and research and he would have a benchmark.

Bibliographies of materials for adults and young adults are numerous. A small personal effort will enable interested persons to uncover many books of interest as well as free materials.

Adair, John J. *Navajo and Pueblo Silversmiths*. Norman, Oklahoma 70369: University of Oklahoma Press, 1954.

——— *A Study of Cultural Resistance: The Veterans of World War II at Zuni Pueblo*. Doctoral Dissertation. Albuquerque, New Mexico 87106: The University of New Mexico, 1948.

Akwesasne Notes. *Voices From Wounded Knee, 1973: The People Are Standing Up*. Akwesasne Publishers. Mohawk Nation. Via Rooseveltown, N.Y. 13683.

——— *BIA - We're Not Your Indians Anymore: The Trail of Broken Treaties and the Twenty Point Program*. Akwesasne Publishers. Mohawk Nation. Via Rooseveltown, N.Y. 13683.

Amsden, Charles Avery. *Prehistoric Southwesterners from Basketmaker to Pueblo*. Los Angeles, 90000: Southwest Museum, 1949.

Bahr, H.M. and others, Eds. *Native Americans Today: Sociological Perspectives*. Harper, New York: 1971.

Bass, Willard P. *The American Indian High School Graduate*. Albuquerque, New Mexico 87106: The Southwestern Cooperative Educational Laboratory for the Bureau of Indian Affairs, 1969.

Belous, Russell E. and Robert A. Weinstein. *Will Soule, Indian Photographer at Fort Sill, Oklahoma, 1869-74.* Los Angeles 90000: Ward Ritchie Press, 1969.

Boyce, George A. *When Navajos Had Too Many Sheep.* Indian Historian Press. San Francisco, 1974.

Brandon, William. *The American Heritage Book of Indians.* New York 10017: Dell Publishing Company, Inc., 1968.

Brody, J.J. *Indian Painters and White Patrons.* University of New Mexico Press: Albuquerque: 1971.

Brophy, William A. and Sophie D. Aberlee. *The Indian: America's Unfinished Business.* Norman 70369: University of Oklahoma Press, 1966.

Brown, D.A. *Bury My Heart at Wounded Knee: An Indian History of the American West.* Holt, New York 1971; Bantam Paper 1972.

Campbell, Maria. *Half Breed.* McClelland and Stewart, Toronto: 1973.

Colden, Cadweller. *The History of the Five Indian Nations: Depending on the Province of New York in America.* Ithaca, New York: Cornell University Press, 1964.

Collier, John. *Indians of the Americas: The Long Hope.* New York: New American Library, Mentor Books, 1947.

Colton, Harold S. *Hopi Kachina Dolls — With a Key to Their Identification.* Albuquerque 87106: University of New Mexico Press, 1959.

Council on Indian Racial Books for Children. *Chronicles of American Indian Protest.* Fawcett Publications. 1973. Greenwich, Conn.

Crochiola, Stanley (Father E.E.). *The Apaches.* Pampa, Texas 79065: Pampa Print Shop, 1962.

_____ *The Jicarilla Apaches of New Mexico.* Pampa, Texas 79065: Pampa Print Shop, 1968.

Curtis, Natalie. ed. *The Indians' Book: Songs and Legends of the American Indians.* New York 10012: Dover Publications, Reprint, 1969, first published 1907.

Deloria, Vine Jr. *Custer Died for Your Sins: An Indian Manifesto.* New York 10012: Macmillan, 1969.

Denig, Edwin Thompson. *Five Indian Tribes of the Upper Missouri: Sioux, Arickaras, Assiniboines, Crees, Crows*. Norman 70369: University of Oklahoma Press, 1961.

Dial, Adolph and David K. Eliades. *The Only Land I Know: A History of the Lumbee Indians*. The Indian Historian Press. San Francisco: 1975.

Dozier, Edward P. *Hano, a Tewan Indian Community in Arizona*. New York: Holt, Rinehart & Winston, 1966.

Driver, Harold E. and Wilhelmine Driver. *Indian Farmers of North America*. New York 10036: Rand McNally Classroom Library, 1967.

_____ *Indians of North America*. Chicago 60637: University of Chicago Press, 1971.

Dunn, Dorothy. *American Indian Painting*. Albuquerque 87106: University of New Mexico Press, 1968.

Ellis, Richard N. *General Pope and the U.S. Indian Policy*. University of New Mexico Press. Albuquerque: 1970.

Farb, Peter. *Man's Rise to Civilization as Shown by the Indians of North America from the Primitive Times to the Coming of the Industrial State*. New York 10012: E.P. Dutton & Co., 1968.

Fergusson, Erna. *Dancing Gods: Indian Ceremonials of New Mexico and Arizona*. Albuquerque 87106: The University of New Mexico Press, 1931.

_____ *New Mexico: A Pagent of Three People*. New York 10012: Knopf, 1951.

Fey, Harold E. and D'Arcy McNickle. *Indians and Other Americans*. New York 10012: Harper & Bros., 1959.

Forbes, Jack D. *Native Americans of California and Nevada*. Healdsburg, Calif.: Naturegraph Press, 1969.

Foreman, Grant. *Indian Removal: The Emigration of the Five Civilized Tribes*. Norman 70369: University of Oklahoma Press, 1953.

Gilpin, Laura. *The Enduring Navajo*. Austin, Texas 78712: University of Texas Press, 1968.

Gookin, Daniel. *Historical Collections of the Indians of New England*. (Reprint Series.) Research Library of Colonial Americana - Richard C. Robey, Gen. Ed. Arno Press. New York: 1972.

Grant, Campbell. *Rock Art of the American Indian.* ISBN Publishers: 1975.

Hagan, William T. *The Indian in American History.* New York 10012: American Historical Association Publication No. 50, 1963.

Hassell, Sandy. *Know the Navajo.* Estes Park, Colorado 80517: printed by Vic Walker, Indian Trader, 1966.

Hertzberg, H.W. *Search For An American-Indian Identity: Modern Pan-American Movements.* Syracuse University Press. Syracuse, N.Y.: 1971.

Hertzberg, Hazel W. *The Great Tree of the Longhouse: The Culture of the Iroquois.* New York 10012: Macmillan Co., 1966.

Hibben, Frank. *The Lost Americans.* New York 10012: Crowell Co., 1946.

Hyde, George E. *Red Cloud's Folk.* Norman 70369: University of Oklahoma Press, 1967.

Index to Literature on the American Indian. Indian Historian Press, Inc. San Francisco, Ca.: 1972.

Johnson, Kenneth M. *K344.* Los Angeles: Dowsi Book Shop (No. 6 in Famous California Trials Series), 1966.

Kaywaykla, James. *In The Days of Victorio: Recollections of a Warm Springs Apache.* University of Arizona Press. 1970.

Kickingbird, Kirke and Karen Ducheneaux, with Forward by Vine Deloria, Jr. *One Million Acres.* MacMillian Co. N.Y.: 1973.

Kilpatrick, Jack Fredrick and Anna Gritts Kilpatrick. eds. *New Echota Letters: Contributions of Samuel Worcester to the Cherokee Phoenix.* Dallas: Methodist University Press, 1968.

Kittler, Glenn D. *Saint in the Wilderness: The Story of St. Jacques and the Jesuit Adventure in the New World.* Garden City, N.Y. 11530: Doubleday, 1964.

Kluckhorn, Clyde and Dorothea C. Leighton. *The Navajo.* Rev. Ed. Garden City, N.Y. 11530: Doubleday & Co., 1962.

Kroeber, A.L. *Handbook of the Indians of California.* Washington, D.C.: Smithsonian Institution (Bureau of Ethnology Publication 78), 1924.

Leighton, Dorothea C. and Clyde Kluckhorn. *The Children of the People.* Cambridge, Mass. 02140: Harvard University Press, 1947.

Levine, Stuart and Nancy O. Laurie. *The American Indian Today*. Deland, Florida: Everett-Edwards, Inc., 1968.

Link, Martin A., Editor. *Navajo — A Century of Progress 1868-1968*. Window Rock, Arizona 86515: K.C. Publications for the Navajo Tribe, 1968.

Longacre, William A. Ed. *Reconstructing Prehistoric Pueblo Societies*. University of New Mexico Press. Albuquerque: 1970.

Macgregor, Gordon. *Warriors without Weapons: A Study of the Society and Personality Development of the Pine Ridge Sioux*. Chicago 60637: University of Chicago Press, 1946.

Mails, Thomas E. *Dog Soldiers, Bear Men and Buffalo Women*. A. & W. Publishers, 1975.

Marriott, Alice. *The First Comers: Indians of America's Dawn*. New York: Longmans, 1960.

_____ *Kiowa Years: A Study in Culture Impact*. (Anthropology Curriculum Study Project) New York: Macmillan Co., 1968.

_____ *These Are The People: Some Notes on the Southwestern Indians*. Santa Fe, N.M. 87501: Laboratory of Anthropology, 1949.

Martin, Paul S., George I. Quimby and Donald Collier. *Indians Before Columbus*. Chicago 60637: University of Chicago Press, 1947.

Marx, Herbert L. Jr., Ed. *The American Indian: A Rising Ethnic Force*. H.W. Wilson Co. New York: 1973.

Maximilian, Prince of Wied. *Travels Into the Interior of North America in the Years 1832 to 1834*. Uncut photo-mechanic reprint of the original two-volume edition of 1839-41 (Coblenze). 1400 pp., ill. 1970. M. & P. Leyh, Printers, D7Stuggart 1, Altenberg-Strasse 38

McCary, Ben C. *Indians in Seventeenth-Century Virginia*. Williamsburgh: Jamestown 350 Anniversary Historical Booklet No. 18, 1957.

Menominee Restoration Efforts. Menominee. P.O. Box 1344, Madison, Wi.: 1973.

Meriam, Lewis. *The Problem of Indian Administration*. Baltimore: Johns Hopkins Press, 1928.

Minnesota Chippewa Indians: A Handbook for Teachers. St. Paul, Minn.: Uppermidwest Regional Educational Laboratory, N.D.

Momaday, Natachee Scott. *American Indian Authors.* Houghton Mifflin, Boston. 1972.

Moquin, Qayne with Charles Van Doren, eds. *Great Documents in American Indian History.* Praeger Publishers. New York: 1973.

National Indian Education Association. *A Guide to Funding Sources for American Library and Information Sources.* National Indian Education Association. 3036 University Avenue, S.E., Minneapolis, Minnesota 55414.

_____ *Index to Bibliographies and Resource Materials.* National Indian Education Association. 3036 University Avenue, S.E., Minneapolis, Minnesota 55414.

Parker, Everett (Two Arrows) and Oledoska (Rising Sun). *The Secret of No Face.* Native American Publishing Co. P.O. Box 2033. Santa Clara, California 95051: 1972.

North, Stanley. *Captured by the Mohawks and Other Adventures by Radisson.* Boston 02107: Houghton, Mifflin, 1960.

Parkman, Francis. *Oregon Trail.* New York 10017: Holt-Rinehart, 1931.

Peterson, Karen Davies, with introduction by John C. Ewers. *Howling Wolf: A Cheyenne Warrior's Graphic Interpretation of His People.* Palo Alto 94306: American West Publishing Co., 1968.

Porter, C. Fayne. *The Battle of the 1,000 Slain.* New York: Scholastic Book Services, 1968.

_____ *Our Indian Heritage: Profiles of 12 Great Leaders.* Philadelphia: Chilton Books, 1964.

Quam, Alvuna. Translator. *The Zunis: Self Portrayals.* (By the Zuni People.) University of New Mexico Press. Albuquerque: 1972.

Roediger, V.M. *Ceremonial Costumes of the Pueblo Indians.* Berkley: University of California Press, Reprint 1961.

Rosen, Kenneth. ed. *The Man To Send Rain Clouds.* Ill. R.C. Gorman and Aaron Yava. Viking Press. New York: 1973.

Schoolcraft, Henry F. *History of the Indian Tribes of the United States: Their Present Condition & Prospects, & A Sketch of Their Ancient Status.* Book Sales Publishers. 1975.

Shorris, Earl. *Death of the Great Spirit: An Elegy for Three American Indians.* Simeon & Schuster, New York: 1971.

Smith, Anne M. *New Mexico Indians: Economic, Educational and Social Problems.* Santa Fe 87501: Museum of New Mexico Research Records No. 1, 1966.

Sonnichsen, C.L. *The Mescalero Apaches.* Norman 70369: University of Oklahoma Press, 1958.

Steiner, Stan. *The New Indian.* New York: Harper & Row, 1968.

Storm, Hyemeyohsts. ed. *Seven Arrows.* Harper. New York: 1972.

Stoutenburgh, John, Jr. *Dictionary of the American Indian.* Philosophical Library. New York: 1960.

Swanton, John R. *The Indians of the Southeastern United States.* Washington, D.C. 20560: Bureau of American Ethnology Bulletin 137, Smithsonian Institute, 1946.

Taylor, Theodore W. *The States and Their Indian Citizens.* U.S. Government Printing Office. Washington, D.C. 20402. Cat. No. 120. 2ST2/3. 1973.

Underhill, Ruth. *Red Man's America: A History of Indians in the United States.* Chicago 60637: The University of Chicago Press, 1953.

United States Commission on Civil Rights. *American Indian Civil Rights Handbook.* (Clearinghouse Publication No. 33) The Commission, Washington, D.C. 20425: n.d.

U.S. Department of the Interior. *Report of the Commissioner of Indian Affairs for the fiscal year ended June 30, 1920.* Washington, D.C. 20402: 1920.

U.S. Department of the Interior, U.S. Geological Survey. *John Wesley Powell and Anthropology of the Canyon Country.* U.S. Geological Survey paper. Washington, D.C. 20402: U.S. Government Printing Office, 1969.

The United States Budget. Washington, D.C. 20520: Office of the Budget Director, various years.

Van Every, Dale. *Disinherited: The Lost Birthright of the American Indian.* New York: William Morrow & Co., 1966.

Waltrip, Lela and Rufus. *Indian Women.* New York: David McKay Co., 1964.

Wetherill, Frances G. and Louisa Wade Wetherill. *Traders to the Navajos: The Story of the Wetherills of Kayenta.* Albuquerque 87106: The University of New Mexico Press, 1953.

White, E.E. *Experiences of a Special Indian Agent.* Norman, Oklahoma 70369: University of Oklahoma Press, 1965.

Wissler, Clark. *Indians of the United States.* Garden City, N.Y. 11530: Doubleday & Co., Rev. Ed. 1966.

Wolf, Robert. *The Dancing Horses of Acoma.* New York: World Publishing Co., 1962.

Yazzie, Etheron, ed. *Navajo History.* Navajo Curriculum Center. Chinle, Az. 86503. Rev. ed. 1974.

NAME INDEX
INDEX TO INDIAN TRIBES AND PROMINENT LEADERS